DIVINE ABUNDANCE

KEYS TO UNLOCK YOUR INNER WISDOM

Aileen Nobles

Light Transformation Publishing Co.
P.O.Box 2826
Malibu, CA 90265
USA

Divine Abundance..........
Keys To Unlock Your Inner Wisdom

Copyright 2001

by

Aileen Nobles

Light Transformation Publishing

PO Box 2826

Malibu, CA, 90265

www.aileennobles.com

First edition published 2001

ISBN: 0-9638102-1-9

Cover photograph by Mara

Acknowledgements

First I would like to say "thank you" to my best friend and wonderful supporter--my husband Fred. Without you this book would never have made it to the bookstores.

Tamara my loving daughter and editor.

Deborah Warren my supportive and patient agent.

Thanks to so many more of you who in various ways encouraged and helped me with the birth of this book. Anne, Elizabeth, Helena, Renee, Pamela, Kathryn, Tamara, Caroline, Wendy, Marion, Tia, Veronica, Kathy, Helene, Carol, Jennifer, Catharine, Sharon. The list of appreciation goes on and on.....and you know who you are.
Thanks as always to my loving Inner Guidance

I love you.

DIVINE ABUNDANCE

KEYS TO UNLOCK YOUR INNER WISDOM

INTRODUCTION

There is a Divine Plan for you. Your life does have a purpose. Abundance is available to you in all areas of your life once you learn the secret of how to live in vibrational harmony with your natural state of Inner Wisdom.

Do these words resonate inside you? Is it really possible to access Divine Abundance? You have a deep Inner Wisdom: experienced as intuition, and it's just waiting for you to consciously connect with it. It's always watching and guiding you much like your Guardian Angel. *And I believe you can not only find it but also directly connect with it!*

How many areas of your life are working for you? Do you feel good even after one of those "not-so-good days? Do you see the perfection in all life as it unfolds? Do you view your life from a position of love and acceptance? Are you in a place of understanding and blessing all you experience? If not, <u>you can be.</u> That is if you choose to be.

Divine Abundance---Keys to Unlock Your Inner Wisdom will show you how to choose this path by introducing you to some simple re-framing techniques. As you learn how to connect with your Inner Wisdom, and open your heart, it becomes possible to embrace

1

and become grateful for everything and everyone in your life. Learn how to change your perspective on the way you view your experiences and gain a greater understanding of the purpose others have in your life, as well.

Once you attune to your Inner Wisdom instead of your ego's perspective, you'll stop reacting against what you don't want or like in your life. Instead, you'll begin to align harmoniously with what you do want. Mastering this basic concept will give you the tools to help change your life forever. And, although it's not magic, the connections you will make and the events and circumstances that you'll draw to yourself will most probably make it appear that way!

All that you want can be yours.

Imagine the possibilities as you learn how to align your energy with all that you desire. You will be able to attract your soulmate who patiently waits in your future, or tap into the vibration of financial abundance. Perhaps you have other desires and dreams such as being healthier, more psychic, finding peace within, or living a more joyful existence. No matter what your dreams, there is a way to align your energy fields with the vibration of everything you dream of having, and,

2

release all attachments to the outcome. As you accomplish this, you will experience an extraordinary sense of well being accompanied by a heightened sense of awareness. You will literally be learning how to co-create your life in harmony with your Inner Guidance system. What a concept!

Understand why up until now, you have not created your life the way you'd prefer it to be. Find out how to connect with your intuition and listen to its guidance. Experience your subconscious, conscious , and superconscious all working together harmoniously to bring you what you want. You will even learn how to re-invent yourself as you connect with a future you. And, you will learn how to allow that newly created self to become your dominant reality.

As you embrace life and all it is offering you, you move into a place of mastery and serenity. From this space of acceptance and gratefulness, align with your Inner Wisdom to co-create the life you want. Your potential is unlimited. If you want it all—you can have it!

Chapter One

BEYOND CREATIVE VISUALIZATION

Wouldn't it be wonderful if you could really understand how you fit into the scheme of things? If you knew how to work "miracles" in creating your life the way you want it to be! For so many of us it appears there has been something we have not quite understood about how to create life the way we want it to be. Maybe you are not even sure whether you really can influence circumstances and events. Perhaps you believe that what happens to you is pot luck, or perhaps fated.

We each want different areas of our life to work better. Your focus may be wanting to experience peace of mind. Perhaps you are looking for someone to love. Maybe your goal is to have an abundant flow of money, or you may want to have more loving friends in your life, or be more creative. Perhaps you just want to feel happier and at peace within yourself. It doesn't matter what you want. We all have wants and don't wants, and if life isn't handing us what we expect, how do we feel? It's so easy to find yourself dissatisfied with what you have, while spending your energy wishing and wanting for something more. Are you still living a life that seems to have so much missing despite all the workshops you have attended, and all the books you have read? Does each day still seem to be a struggle even though you meditate and consciously work on yourself?

The power of creative energy is available
for everyone to harness and utilize

Quantum physicists such as Albert Einstein have proven what metaphysicians have been saying for years. All we perceive in our universe that appears to be solid, is actually made up of vibrating energy. Everything that we think of that makes up our physical universe whether it is our car, our body, money, or our home is actually made up of atomic particles of energy. Atoms are made up of subatomic particles, which are fluctuations of energy, and impulses of information. In other words not solid. Everything that you can think of in your life has a vibration and a frequency and is made out of particles of energy. A solid wall is in fact, not solid. An open space like the sky, is in fact not open, but filled with many tiny particles of light and substance. This includes your physical body and your thoughts. Our bodies are mostly made up of space filled with atoms and subatomic particles of energy. We literally are energy beings, in fact everything in the universe is vibrating particles of energy emitting a vibration. A quantum is a packet of light–light that is made up of particles and waves. A quantum field is where everything is connected to everything else. Every thought you have also sends out its own vibration, its own frequency, and affects all that it connects with.

We tend to believe that an object that we can see and feel that belongs to our outer world, is more real and important in many ways than a thought, feeling, or a sense of intuition that is connected to our inner world All thoughts are impulses of energy that are not only created in our heads but make up our universe. Both our inner and outer worlds are made up of pulsating vibrations of energy. It is the speed of the vibration that determines whether they are visible or invisible, yet both play an important role in our lives. It is your inner senses that pick up vibrations of such a high frequency that you cannot see them. But even though you cannot visibly see them, these waves of energy are just as real as the objects that you can see and touch. No one denies that television and radio waves exist, and yet thought waves are really no different.

Imagine for a moment that you are seeing yourself and all that is around you as particles of energy ever moving, changing and transforming themselves. This gives a different perspective than you would have if you thought of your world as a solid mass of animate and inanimate objects. What if your thoughts could actually create movement of this invisible energy that is within, through and around your body?

Believe me, you are more than you think you are

Have you ever entertained the idea that there is more to you than is apparent on the surface? Is it possible that you are not simply a physical being learning to become more spiritual, that perhaps you are primarily a being of spirit in a physical body? When I refer to a "spiritual being or spiritual path" it has nothing to do with religious beliefs. My feelings about being spiritual are connected with a love of Source, and a desire to become the most unconditionally loving and joyful person that I am capable of being.

What do I mean by saying that perhaps you are a "spiritual being" in a human body? The energy that makes up our universe on a subatomic particle level moves within us as well as all around us. We are not separate from it, and it is not ours–it belongs to–and is a part of all beings, it is eternal and universal.

This powerful Source Energy is all loving, non-judgmental, and always creating.

It is the reason why our planet orbits and the sun rises and sets. It is why the rain waters the plants and trees and why the birds sing. It is what allows us to breathe without even thinking about it, and it is the breath of Source as we inhale that becomes a part of who we are. This Source energy within us acts as an Inner Wisdom, and if it is not blocked by our past experiences and beliefs, connects us to joy, peace and love. As I write this book I am working with the understanding that most people believe in some type of Higher Intelligence or Creative Power which is the source of all that exists in our universe. I will be using the term "Source" as I refer to this energy, but feel free to substitute "God" or any other word that allows you to feel comfortable. The words "Inner Guidance" and "Inner Wisdom" are used to refer to this Source energy. Even though this energy resides within all of us, the majority think of themselves only in physical terms. If your identity has been mostly determined by how you look and what you have accomplished, you probably believe the outside world offers you more of everything that allows you to feel better. This includes the search for meaning in your life. On the other hand, if you are open enough to accept that you are part of Source Energy, you will sense that you have the answer to your happiness within you.

No matter what your beliefs, over the years you may have already tried various ways to manifest your desires and dreams, only to lose hope as the techniques you used didn't appear to work. You held a vision, focused on it daily, and even put it into words. Diligently you practiced your affirmations waiting for your dream to materialize, yet your life didn't seem to change, and you were not able to understand why. I ask you for a moment now, to act as if you have no preconceived ideas about how you think things are, and to pretend instead that you are ready to open your mind to new possibilities.

Now....read on.

There are a number of reasons for apparent failure of your affirmations and visualization, and you will soon begin to understand what was missing. When you say your affirmations it is important to say them with energy and desire, and not just repeat them without passion and intensity. Your word alone does not contain the energy and vibrational frequency necessary for magnetic attraction. It is the energy and passion behind the words you say that make the difference. Your thoughts set up the vision of what you want to create. Your emotions energize the thought and send it from your inner world into the outer world where it will connect with similar vibrations of energy. When enough energy of similar vibration comes together, matter is created, and becomes an event or object or experience in your life. Always remember that the energy of the thought is far more powerful than any spoken word. Unless the word has a strong emotional charge attached to it, you may simply not be generating enough emotional feeling to effect manifestation.

What if everything you could ever imagine is already at your fingertips, waiting for you to harmonize with its vibration.

As you read these words, what thoughts flash through your mind? Could it be possible? And if it is, why does there seem to be so much lack in the world? Why haven't your affirmations and visualizations brought you what you wanted?

To understand how magnetic attraction works, it may be easier for you to think about your thoughts as if they were magnets that attract a similar magnetic vibration. All our energetic thoughts flow out into the universe, find their equal match in vibration and quality, and return to us more of the same. This type of attraction is being played out in our lives daily.

How many times have you thought of an old friend or neighbor. You wonder how they are doing, and you think how nice it would be to have contact with them again. Perhaps you have not seen them for a while. Later that day you receive a phone call from them, or someone will mention their name, or you may even bump into them on the street. This seeming coincidence occurred, because as you thought about that person you sent out an energy. Your focused thought connected with a matching energy and created circumstances to give you what you were thinking about. It makes no difference whether your thoughts are positive or negative. They are equally magnetic, as shown in the following example.

If you find yourself continually thinking about what is wrong with the world, your energy will attract negative situations. You may hear heated arguments on the streets, or perhaps you will pick relationships filled with a lot of negativity that tend to validate your thoughts. With daily repetition, these thoughts will multiply through their magnetic attraction and become a foundation for your brain's belief system. Like a tiny trickle of water which manages to carve out an area as immense as the Grand Canyon over eons of time, your thoughts carve out your own energy patterns through constant repetition. Consciously and subconsciously, they will bring to you whatever you have focused on.

Likewise, if you place your focus on peaceful and harmonious, situations, you will attract circumstances into your life where people are kind to you, go out of their way to smile at you, or perhaps offer some kind of helpful service.

I have seen for example, that people who have experienced physical abuse tend to see much more violence on the streets than I do. It is only after I realize that we walk the same streets, that I understand that it is not a particular area that breeds this negativity. It is our different beliefs and thoughts towards hostility that determine through our vibration what we attract into our lives, and experience in the world.

Since violence is not now or has ever been a large part of my experience, I don't often think or speak about it, and therefore I don't resonate with the energy patterns it generates. It doesn't mean that violence does not exist, because everything exists in the world.

Indeed, everything exists in the entire universe at the same time, but rather I don't tune in to the frequency of violence, and therefore do not attract it into my daily life.

This would change, however, if I begin to watch television shows filled with angry people, or start to believe that people are inherently rude, mean or spiteful. Possibly I might even act out negative thoughts and begin to quarrel with others, or become extremely fearful. If I tune in to the energy of violence, or become overly fearful of being around violence, I would be sending out a vibration that attracts violence into my experience. I know that I would instantly begin to see a correlation to this new belief in the situations of the world around me.

My focus on anger would magnetically attract more of the same to me. The universe would present me with exactly what I had asked for through my thoughts and the attention I had given to them. I would indeed begin to see, and have presented to me a greater awareness of the existence of anger everywhere. These experiences would then offer me exactly what I needed to look within, release what I do not want, and by doing so accelerate my growth and awareness.

*Through your thoughts and emotions you
are literally deciding throughout each day the
state of your present and future life*

Are you focussed on not having found your soulmate, or worrying about not having enough money to
pay your bills, or envisioning yourself as a sick person?
If you are you will begin to see yourself as a victim and
fall into the "oh poor me syndrome." But, remember
these thoughts you are having are flowing outward
adding to themselves, and then returning more of the
same to you. You are creating your future right now!
The impartial universe does not differentiate between
"I want ice cream, or I don't want ice cream," Either
way the universe will support your wanting, and you
will continue to want!

It's time to become the gatekeeper of your thoughts
and emotions. Indeed, until now, you may have been
completely unaware just how very important and powerful your thoughts are!

There is no rule that says that the changes you
desire in your life cannot happen quickly, for the speed
is determined almost solely by your intent and intensity of thought. The energy and passion you generate
while affirming, will determine how quickly your
desires materialize. Just as how often and with what

intensity you exercise determines the rate in which you build muscle, the speed of manifestation is directly determined by how clear and aligned you are.

Every thought you have with passion and intensity is finding its equal matchand returning more of the same to you.

In other words you are responsible for all that you have attracted into your life! What a wake up call. Now that you know this, ask yourself "What kind of thoughts am I thinking"? "What emotions am I feeling?" For you are always thinking and feeling thoughts about something or someone, so are you creating what you want or what you don't want?

As you read this, are your thoughts and feelings creating the type of future that will uplift you, or are you unconsciously creating more of the "same old thing" and then complaining that your life doesn't seem to improve? This idea of being responsible for everything you are experiencing, may at first be a little hard for you to accept. As it becomes a possibility in your mind you will also realize that it means you have some control over your life. It means that if you want different experiences, it's possible for you to have them.

***What you hold in consciousness right now is
creating a future event for you.***

Everyday with your thoughts and emotions, you
are creating something in your life that *will* manifest in
your future. Because you are a part of the energy of the
universe, you are in constant creation: yet, rarely are
you aware of what your "thought energy" has created
that *will* become a part of your life.

Its frightening to think that most of our thoughts
are subconscious or unconscious, and we are not even
aware of most of our conscious thoughts. Daily, our
minds run and rerun so many of the same old patterns,
often focusing on problems, insecurities, fears, sadness
and anger. Thoughts that bring us down instead of lift-
ing us up. We keep re-writing the same old script and
wonder why we don't feel better.

If we are always creating something with our
thoughts, it becomes apparent how important it is to
watch what we are thinking. We then have the option
to change our thoughts if they are focused on what we
do <u>not</u> want. As you accept responsibility for all that is
in your life you truly empower yourself to discover
your higher purpose. By doing so, you will connect
with a flow of universal energy that guides you to manifest abundance in all areas that are important to you.

Tamara is a delightful example of how to manifest a dream. For a number of years she had worked in the world of film as a coordinator, and at other times worked in the special effects department. For most people this would seem like a dream come true, yet for Tamara she had another dream. She loved to create beauty and wanted to have her own home to fix up, make it beautiful, and then sell it. Tamara did not have the finances for this type of venture yet did not focus on that aspect of her situation at all. After work she would cruise areas where there were little old houses that needed to be fixed up and she finally found one that really appealed to her. As she told me her story her eyes were lit up and she was living her excitement. She climbed a fence to stand inside this old deserted house and walked around imagining how it was going to look when she had fixed it up. She returned to this house three times, each time with this knowing inside that this is how she wanted to spend her time. She was sure this type of work would make her heart and soul sing. She had no idea how she could possibly buy a house as she didn't have any savings. She decided she needed an investor.

One day Tamara was at a fund raising dinner with her parents. She was not sure she wanted to attend, but she knew it would make her father happy. At the dinner table she started talking to the person next to her. It turned out that his wife enjoyed interior design and he was looking to invest in properties to fix up and sell. The outcome of her clear and focused desire ended up with her investor putting the house in her name, and her dreams became a reality.

Tamara did not let other people tell her that she was making a mistake to leave a financially secure position with the film industry. She did not put herself around anyone who had negative feelings or experiences they wanted to share with her. She stayed focused on her dream, and so the universe created synchronistic events that led to her dream becoming a reality. I know this story is true, for she is my daughter.

Every time you imagine what you want, you may also be sending out an opposing thought that cancels out the manifestation of your desire.

Another reason that you may not have had the success you wanted is because you are sending out conflicting energies. As you do your creative visualization and affirmations, be aware of any negative thoughts you may be generating simultaneously. The energy of any negative thoughts might just have counteracted your positive thinking!

So, practicing creative visualization, affirmations and positive thinking, without understanding the subconscious programming of your beliefs, will probably not create the results you are looking for. If you desire something consciously and it aligns with your superconscious, then it will further your Soul growth. You will expect to feel energized and happy inside as you think these thoughts. Yet if you have a subconscious thought that is in conflict, something will feel amiss as you do your visualizations.

Let's say, for example, you have the conscious thought that you want to be with a wonderful soulmate for the rest of your life. If you feel no resistance to the idea of wanting this special relationship, you will feel expansive and powerful as you think about creating this connection.

If, however, you are thinking at the same time, "Yes, that's what I want, but how many good men or women are there out there. Or, "most of them cannot be trusted." "They are all gold diggers." "Who would want me anyway." Or even, "It's not possible to have a long happy marriage because I know most marriages fail." Be aware that all of these beliefs carry their own energy. You will be sending out the vibration of negative feelings on the tail end of the positive vibration of

"I want a wonderful soulmate." And, because the happy thought has a quicker vibration than the pessimistic thought they are not in harmony, and cancel each other out. Therefore, it is possible that nothing you are affirming happens.

Its easier to see your conscious thoughts and how they connect with your experiences but you now have to bring your subconscious thoughts into consciousness. This is a little more tricky. Perhaps you have a subconscious thought that you are not even aware of keeping you from love. If your parents were unhappy, or a dear friend had a difficult divorce you may have vowed that you were not going to put yourself in a similar position. To your literal subconscious (that doesn't think) that may have been interpreted as: "I won't ever fall in love and become that vulnerable." So to protect yourself you don't seem to meet Mr. or Ms. Wonderful, and you don't even know why!

When life is not going the way we want it to, we tend to spend a lot of time thinking about the way we want it to be. We also spend a lot of time thinking about what is wrong, with one thought very quickly following the other. Perhaps you want a promotion, and you really believe that it's time for you to have one. You have paid your dues, worked hard, been reliable and honest and it definitely is your turn. Right behind that thought you might be thinking how you do not seem to get the credit you deserve. Perhaps your boss seems to favor someone else over you. Your co-workers Joe or Suzy also want a promotion, and it wouldn't surprise you if one of them received it instead of you. In fact you may almost talk yourself into believing that you will not get the promotion. And, quite possibly it will not happen. Why? Because as you think the positive thoughts about being ready and right for a promotion, if it feels good as you say it, the universe is beginning to re-arrange itself to bring you what you want. Right behind that energy you are also sending out another energy based on fear. Fear and anxiety are the opposite of what you want to manifest, yet the universe is also re-arranging itself responding to your focus. What happens, is that the two opposing emotional vibrations will cancel each other out and probably nothing in your work situation will change. You won't know what went wrong, and may end up feeling like a victim.

As you think about what you want in your life,
the universe is rearranging itself around your
thoughts so that your desires become manifested.

Another example: Perhaps you are thinking about moving to a larger home. You may have a very strong desire to move. Or perhaps you are pregnant and need another bedroom for the new baby, or you need more room for an office at home. Perhaps you just want more space to move around in so that you don't feel so cramped. As you think about what you want, you can picture the type of house or apartment that would be best for you. You can even capture the feelings of excitement you have as you imagine yourself in a larger wonderful new home. As you think about it you feel really good. Now, what thoughts might be right behind your vision. Maybe thoughts of "well that would be wonderful, but I can't afford to pay a higher mortgage or rent." Or, "if I move, what will happen if I don't have enough income to afford a bigger home. What will happen if I lose my job. Or, suppose one of us gets sick, and we have large doctor bills to pay, how will we afford to do it all?" The idea of the first thought about the home you want is traveling out into the universe. The energy of the universe is beginning to rearrange itself around that desire--until the next idea of not enough money was released. These thoughts are not harmonious with each other, and the result is that you'll probably not be moving in the near future.

Now think about the difference in feelings that you experienced. As you had your first thought of "I want a new home," you felt excited, good and energetic as you connected with that vision. The universe wants to give you whatever you imagine is beneficial to you, and your desire had a high vibration that was clear. The next thought was one of lack, and as you thought about not having enough, you didn't feel good. That thought was not vibrationally in harmony with your desire. Your uncomfortable feelings were letting you know that you were creating more lack as you entertained those thoughts.

My own house story is a classic example of what can be accomplished with a clear and trusting focus. About fifteen years ago I was living with my husband and daughter in a small house that we were renting in Pacific Palisades. For years they had both put up with me talking about the wonderful huge house we would have over looking the ocean. In my imagination I had decided long ago that I would live the way I wanted to live in the house of my dreams and nobody could talk me out of it.

I started driving out to Malibu looking around at various houses. One day I came across an empty house that was enclosed by a wire fence. My heart started beating faster, and an odd sense of excitement swept over me. I crawled under the fence and walked around this house that overlooked the ocean, and peeked into every window I could find. It was large and beautiful, and it even had a swimming pool. Everything about the house was telling me that even if the owner wanted to lease it out, it would be far more money than we could ever afford. As usual that thought didn't seem to be important. When my family came home I talked my husband, daughter and dog into taking a ride up to see our future house. As we all crawled under the fence, they thought I was crazy to believe we could ever afford to live there, but they humored me.

I visited the house many times sitting outside overlooking the ocean. And while meditating I simply sat saying "thank you" for the house instead of wondering how I was going to get it. A few weeks later a friend called to say she had heard about a house in Malibu that was going to be rented out by a new owner. It had been vacant for five years due to the threat of landslides. I called the owner and he gave me the address to meet him to see the house.

Well, you probably guessed by now that it was my dream house. He told me how much the lease was, and I told him how much we could pay! I also mentioned my story to him about how I found the house, and that from the moment I saw it I knew I was to live in it. Now I can happily say that I have been living here in paradise for nearly fifteen years. Miracles do happen!

This story illustrates the power of a clear, unwavering focus. Most of the time when you think about what you want in life and how you want your life to be you are thinking conflicting thoughts, completely unaware that you are doing it. All you know is that your visualizing and prayers do not seem to be answered a lot of the time. The trick is to know how to focus on what you desire and then visualize and affirm it in a congruent way. If you feel balanced, your emotions match your thoughts, and your subconscious, conscious and superconscious are all in agreement. If you feel uncomfortable, on some level you have conflicting thoughts.

If you start imagining what you want at a time when you are very conscious of what you don't have, you may experience feeling heavy, slow, or depressed. The time that you start affirming and visualizing and praying is usually when you are in a situation that seems to be the opposite of what would make you happy. You may be feeling sad or angry, fearful or anxious. Doesn't it make sense to try and change your life at that moment? It always did to me, until I realized that in that feeling of struggle I was not at all clear. In fact I only seemed to get more stuck, and the feelings I was trying to get rid of only strengthened.

Whenever I am in an anxious emotional state, I know that I am not attuned to my Inner Wisdom. Although I am trying to co-create, I am not in a place of feeling that the abundance of the universe is available to me. I may say the right words but I don't really believe them. I am trying to get what I want from a desperate feeling, and, without fail I only create more struggle.

Whenever you are sending out thoughts and especially emotional thoughts that are pushing against "what is," instead of sending out thoughts to create what you want, the universe is responding to your focus on what you don't want. And you will receive more of it! When you are focused on what is missing or what you want to change, you are vibrationally attuned to lack and need. You are probably also feeding yourself negative self-defeating talk. You are listening to your ego/personality at this point and may be feeling that it is foolish to try and pretend that you can really have an effect on what is happening in your life.

While experiencing these types of thoughts and emotions the molecules of your body are vibrating at a slower frequency. As they are not in harmony with what you wish to create, there is a mismatch of energy. You can recognize when this is happening, as it creates an uncomfortable emotional feeling within. The more sensitive you become to your feelings, the more you can consciously control your thoughts and emotions.

You must realize that every hidden agenda you carry, whether you are aware of it or not, will greatly affect your ability to manifest your desires. In this book I will show you how to ferret out the part of you that perhaps feels unworthy, or believes in limitation. You will find out how to replace it with a working understanding of the basic principles of thought and energy, so that you can, and will, create what appear to be miracles.

The universe constantly rearranges
itself around your thoughts, words, emotions
and your visions of reality.

If you ready to start manifesting consciously, you need to become more sensitive to your your feelings. The easiest way is to find some quiet time to just be still, turn within and listen with your whole being.

Feelings are like road maps, and as the majority of us struggle to manage our lives, many seem to be sorely out of touch with this constant inner guidance. Your feelings are a barometer that are always letting you know if you are thinking something uplifting or something that is depressing. You sometimes may feel like a car traveling down a one way street, unsure of your direction, yet without the understanding and guidance to interpret signs which might show you a detour or offer you a chance to turn around. Your feelings are these signposts, and without them, you often travel unmarked routes, feeling cut off from your Source, and unable to imagine yourself having love, joy, health and abundance in your everyday life at all.

So, to be told that you already have access to everything you could ever dream of, is sometimes a world away from the reality you are choosing to live. But the word choosing is very deliberate, for you do choose what you experience in life, through your conscious or even unconscious continuous flow of thoughts.

When you focus on what is wrong in your life
the impartial universe goes out of its way
to give you more of what you are focusing on.

So why is it that you have tried so many techniques yet still they haven't worked? Take a look at your own life. Think about where your focus and thoughts are for a good portion of the day. You may be surprised to observe that most of your day is focused on all that you don't have. You may worry about what is missing, challenging or difficult, often spending hours thinking about what is wrong. Sometimes you may hold this negative focus so intensely that you exclude the thoughts of all that you do have. Often you may completely forget how much there is in your life for which you can be grateful.

Remember that your thoughts as energy are magnetic, so when you focus on what is missing, you get more of the same. If you are full of anxiety and worry about issues in your life, then you are setting yourself up to perpetuate these feelings and emotions that are so uncomfortable to live with. You also find yourself resisting what is in your life that you don't want, therefore perpetuating it. You will definitely benefit from consciously choosing to change your focus. For, as you send out thoughts of what you want,

29

believing that it already exists on an energy level, the universe responds.

You have a built in guidance system.

Sometimes as you go about your daily routine, do you find yourself feeling frustrated and impatient? Are you aware that you are not living up to your potential--even if you are not sure what your potential might be? Perhaps you are not sure what capabilities and gifts you possess, if any! You wonder if there is a Divine Plan in the universe that includes your life, and, if there is, why are you still searching for it?

Imagine for a moment (whether you believe it or not) that you have available to you a guidance system that has an overview of your Divine Plan. A guidance system of Inner Wisdom that is directly connected with your Higher Self. As you accept this concept, your focus begins to move away from looking to the outer world for your answers, happiness, and purpose in life. You begin to realize that it really is possible that you have everything you are looking for available already, and its up to you to connect with it. How futile to spend so much of your life looking everywhere for someone else to wave the magic wand, when it is actually right here within you. Not outside of you. It is YOU!

Do you ever think that you have an infinitely wiser part of you? Have you ever allowed for the possibility that there is a part of you that might have a higher perspective, an overview of life that the "everyday" you has not yet connected with? It's very exciting to take on a broader view of what you might be able to do in your life when you connect with your untapped resources.

As you connect with your intuition, you are
connecting with a clearer part of yourself
that is your guiding force--your Inner Wisdom.

As you think about what you want in life, through your intuitive feelings you will know if you are creating something that is in your best interest. If you feel a positive flow of energy, know that your choices are aligned with your soul's growth, and your Inner Wisdom. As you attune to that clear flow of energy, you will find yourself filled with a clarity and ease that allows you to live your life fully and joyfully without struggle.

Throughout your day, watch your emotionally charged thoughts, and see how these thoughts translate into feelings. Notice your sense of contentment or unease, and decide which belief system you are connecting to the experience you are having. If you notice uncomfortable feelings, be aware of how much energy you are using up by pushing against what you don't want. That same energy can be used to positively create a vision of what you do want. Let your emotions be a barometer to show you which facets of your life might benefit from improvement.

Think about an area of your life where you have struggle. An area that you desperately want to be different. You may have abundance financially but lack loving friendships in your life. Or, you may have financial abundance, yet be in ill health. Perhaps you are bursting with good health but have a struggle with earning enough money to live life the way you choose. As you look around, you might notice that very few people seem to have everything they want, and even fewer seem to be joyful and content. Pay attention to how often you think about not having all that you want. How strongly do you feel lack in a particular area? Every time you focus on what is missing or wrong you are creating unconsciously, attracting more of what you do not want.

Think of a time when you really knew what you wanted. It was clear in your mind. You had a visual image of it. As you thought about having or doing it, you felt uplifted. That positive feeling you felt within happens when you passionately want something and are vibrating in harmony with it. At those times have you noticed how everything seems to flow, and whatever you focus on accomplishing somehow happens without much effort. Life sometimes seems so perfectly choreographed—and it is!

This example of co-creating is conscious creation, yet you are creating so much of your life unconsciously. When you are not aware of your thoughts and beliefs that adversely impact your life, you unconsciously set up situations for yourself that are perfect for you to learn from. You may not always like the circumstances and situations you find yourself in, yet they are exactly what you need at the moment. If you didn't need them they wouldn't be part of your experience. In other words, you are like a magnet. Anything inside you that needs strengthening or healing, carries a vibration to match the emotion.

The Divine Plan of your unfolding is so perfect that you only attract what can help you with the next stage of your growth.

Whatever you find yourself experiencing is with you for a reason, for your thoughts, conscious or unconscious have bought it to you. If everything in the universe is made up of the same energy, that means all the things you judge to be bad as well as the things you are happy with are from the same source. As you look around you begin to see that if everything is part of the Divine Intelligence, and you accept that, then everything is as its meant to be.

The universe is on purpose.
Source doesn't make mistakes.

You may like some things in your life more than others. You are happier with some people and circumstances and not so happy with others, yet, all is as it's meant to be. Everything is in your life because on some level you need it. You may not understand why you need it. It may be very unpleasant at times and very difficult to take an overview. Yet knowing what you don't want will allow you to see more clearly what you do want.

Your feelings are always determined by your thoughts about your life. They are attached to beliefs that decide whether you are going to be happy or unhappy, calm or anxious, loving or vindictive. Your thinking is often based on habit, and repeating old patterns, yet thinking thoughts that create a reality you don't want can be changed. You do have a choice about how you view life, and the more aware you are of how your beliefs affect your thinking, the easier it is to clear the ones that no longer serve you. If we are responsible for <u>all</u> we are co-creating, it is very clear to me that I would rather be thinking thoughts that are in harmony with my soul, than struggle with difficult and challenging situations that I have created for myself by listening to my emotions and ego.

Think again of a situation or area of your life where you are successful. It may be connected with health, love or affluence. It will probably be an area that you expect to run smoothly. Your thoughts when you focus on this part of your life are mostly positive, and you expect everything to continue to work out the way you want. If you think about it, you will notice that you spend very little time focused on what is not working. As you expect the best, you think thoughts in harmony with your Inner Guidance. Subsequently, that creates good feelings when you think about that particular area of your life.

WHAT'S MISSING?

If you are now entertaining the possibility that you have created everything that's in your life, it's time to review what you have attracted. The best way to do this is from a detached overview which will give you a different perspective than a purely emotional one. As you start this process ask to be filled with the flow of Divine Energy that is always present. Focus on an area of your life that you struggle with, and decide not to judge it, or yourself. Rather, try to look at your life as an observer, or, as a benevolent outside party would.

Perhaps your chosen area is finance. As hard as you work you never seem to have enough money to do more than pay your bills–or perhaps not enough to even pay them. For others of you your focus may be on relationships, and you may feel so alone in your life without someone special to love. Or you may feel depressed, not fully alive. Whatever area you are struggling with is the way you have created it! Yes, you have set up these circumstances probably unconsciously, programmed by your beliefs about life. Beliefs that are accepted by you as truth. Perhaps they aren't even yours originally, yet they create great stress and limitation in your life. Isn't it time to take a look and release whatever beliefs no longer serve you?

As you become more aware, you accept that you are here on earth for a purpose. You realize that your life is not happening by accident. You were not randomly dropped by the stork into your family. In fact everything in your life especially the parts that are not flowing smoothly, are all showing you a way to become more whole. Sometimes, you bring these challenges with you from past lives, which does make it harder to release them. However, it doesn't make it impossible. Whatever you don't have that you want, is the very thing that you are not allowing to flow to you. You are literally pushing it away from coming into your experience to the degree that you do not have it!

You have probably created all sorts of rationalizations and excuses as to why you're not living the life you want. Often this will include blaming someone else for your woes, after all, its so much easier than taking full responsibility for your painful life situations.

Remember, that all your thoughts and doubts that are getting in the way of creating the life you want need to be cleared, but, how are you going to do that? You can never get rid of something by thinking about getting rid of it. Another approach is needed. For as you think about getting rid of something, the universe picks up on your focus and you get more of what your trying to erase–creating more struggle.

*Knowing what you don't want is the
quickest route to show you what you do want*

Once you really look at an area of your life that is
not abundant, whether in love, finance, happiness or
health, you're getting ready to make a decision about
what you do want. Struggle is Source offering you a
choice with a wake up call. How long do you want to
suffer and perpetuate your struggle by blaming others
and life. Isn't it time to look at your options, suspend
your old limiting beliefs and try something new?

Everything in your life whether you consciously
want it or not, is a vibrational match to the energy you
have been sending out. You have created it all! Your
limitations <u>are</u> all your own doing. If you find that a
large part of your life is a struggle, somewhere in your
conscious or subconscious mind you will be holding
on to a belief that says you expect it to be that way.
Over the years, you may have heard and accepted from
many people important to you that "life is a struggle."
Every time you found yourself in a challenging situation you probably thought about how difficult life is.
There would be a lot of energy behind this thought as
perhaps you were thinking it when you were feeling
overwhelmed, exhausted or anxious. The universe just
picks up on the energy of your thought and gives you

more of what you are focusing on--so the struggle continues. This type of thinking becomes a habit. The quicker you see your negative thoughts, the quicker you can change your pattern.

LIMITATIONS ACCEPTED AS TRUTH

What about your belief in limitation? Have you spent enough years of your life believing how limited you are? Accepting that you have very little control over your life. Have you constantly talked about what is wrong, focusing on what's missing? Are you still blaming others, and making them the reason you haven't yet got your life together? It's your mothers fault because of the way she brushed her teeth. Its your fathers fault because he abandoned you at a crucial point in your life. Its your brothers fault because he pinched you when no one was looking. Blame stunts your growth and gives you a reason why you haven't got your life together. Its time to move on. The longer you talk and think about the evils of the world, the longer you will be experiencing them.

It's better to become a visionary and believe that all will be well, holding positive outcomes in your mind. You may find as you express optimism to others, that unless you are very aware of who you talk to, you will receive some negative feedback. We all seem to have parents, relatives or well meaning friends who are constantly nipping our dreams in the bud. I remember hearing so often the words " You spend too much time daydreaming. Your hopes are just pie in the sky, you need to get back to reality."

I was luckier than most, for nobody stopped me from dreaming of what I wanted to have or to do. My inner knowing kept me co-creating even if at such a young age I was not conscious of what I was doing. I decided very early on that nobody was going to tell me what I could or couldn't have, or what was possible or impossible. I walked to the beat of my own drummer. Now I realize that walking to the beat of a different drummer is definitely a necessary part of "waking up." It is an important step in reclaiming your power, enabling you to move away from non-productive limiting thoughts. Thoughts that would have you believe that you are a victim of your destiny, or the system. Indeed, believing in limitations set by society can make you feel so weak and helpless, that you completely shut yourself off from your higher clearer part that is always wanting you to recognize your unlimited potential.

*To create your own reality, make space
for your dreams to come true.*

Limiting thoughts definitely do not feel harmonious. Your body and emotions let you know immediately that your thoughts are not beneficial to you, and will not attract what you want. What you do get by focusing on what you "don't have," or "don't expect to achieve," is exactly that, more of not having. You find yourself feeling more and more powerless to change circumstances and events in your life. Often it appears that the harder you try the worse it gets.

If, for one moment you really believe that you cannot change your thoughts into a more positive framework, you are buying into powerlessness. Remember that the universe is constantly rearranging itself around your beliefs. You and the universe are pure energy in constant motion. You do have a choice. You can make a decision right now to let go of your limiting baggage of thoughts that have held you back up to this point. You can start in this moment to release all thoughts that are keeping you stuck.

Let us take an example of, "I didn't go to college, or "I didn't get my Ph.D. therefore my ability to generate income is limited." Ask yourself, "is that really true, or have I simply accepted what someone else said as a reason to feel limited and not achieve my true potential?"

When you ask yourself that question you may hear your personality answer. "Yes its true, look at how little you have accomplished up to now, always goofing off and procrastinating or perhaps accepting jobs that are not challenging you." Now become quiet, and ask your Inner Wisdom if it's really true. As you attune you will hear the loving support that encourages you to find a dream and believe in it. The inner voice that says you can accomplish anything if you follow your heart and soul. Magic is there for you if you find something that you have a talent for that gives you great pleasure

A wonderful example of success would be Thomas Edison. He didn't have a higher education, and, it was because of his deafness caused by his father boxing his ears, that he pursued his interest in communications. A few other success stories are: Colonel Sanders, founder of Kentucky Fried Chicken, and Amos of Famous Amos cookies. They found something they enjoyed doing, that they were good at, and they followed their dreams.

Education is a tool to enhance your ability , and is very necessary if your goal requires a degree. Even more powerful is a strong desire to pursue your dreams, using your voice of intuition as a guide. Education is wonderful, but don't let your lack of conventional schooling limit your belief in yourself and your abilities.

Release your limiting beliefs and set yourself free.

Toni was a wonderful example of what can happen if you let go of limiting thoughts. When I first met Toni, she had been feeling very frustrated and sad. She had come to the realization later in life that she wanted to have a baby. She and her husband had been trying half heartedly to conceive for over a year. They had adopted the idea that if it happened then it was meant to be, yet had not really allowed themselves to think that it was the "right" thing to do. She had very firmly accepted the idea that she was too old to conceive, and would not be able to be a "good" mother because of her age.

Toni had been a very successful business woman and had accomplished almost everything she had put her mind to. Yet here she was accepting the limiting thought that she should not have a baby.

We connected with her Inner Guidance and she asked this part of herself if it was really true that she was too old, or was it just a belief she had accepted. Her inner answer was far more true than the denial of her desires. She had been listening to what others believed to be "right" for her. Opinions that were based on their own limitations and beliefs.

When Toni gave herself permission to imagine being a wonderful mother, she became pregnant within a few months of our session. As one would expect, she is now a dynamic and loving mother supporting her baby to be all that he can be—without limitations!

Chapter Two

YOUR HIDDEN AGENDAS

If you don't have everything you ever dreamed of, ask yourself why not? Why doesn't every day feel like a birthday? Why is your bank account not overflowing with unlimited zeros behind the numbers? Why are you not living with the love of your life?

Thoughts alone are simply energy. However, the beliefs that you attach to those thoughts then create a positive or negative charge. And these charges—be they positive or negative—are determined by your prior judgments and past experiences. Your thoughts then, are formed in response to and are biased by your own past. Most often than not, they're also a detriment to creating clarity in the present moment. Carrying these past beliefs does not support the life you are ready to create. Instead they are part of a hidden agenda that manifests conflict in your life. These hidden beliefs are the reason that your creative visualization and affirmations don't necessarily work.

We all have different backgrounds, and there are numerous reasons why you may not be sending out energy in harmony with your desires. This is doubly frustrating, as you may be diligently working at creating what you want. Yet, beliefs about who you are, how powerful you are (or are not) or how unworthy you are, all serve as double messages to the universe. These are some of the reasons why your life does not change according to your desires.

- You may *think* that you believe life has unlimited joys to offer, but you may actually have programmed yourself to accept the opposite.

- You may tell yourself that you are ready to receive the abundance from the universe. Yet, if there's a little voice in your head saying, "that's not how life is," or, "look around and see how much suffering and poverty there is," or "it can't be that easy," you have conflicting beliefs. That "little" voice is the most powerful one, and that's the message you're sending out to the universe. The strongest voice, that "little' voice, is the one that will bring you what you do not want!

- You may consciously believe you are ready to create what you desire, but may have a subconscious belief that is working against you.

We often make our lives harder than necessary. Many of us have bought into the concept that before we're able to do or feel what we want--to have happiness and security in our lives, for example–we first need to be financially secure. It's as if our lives go on hold until we have created enough money to buy our freedom and security. Trying to *make* things happen, is the opposite energy of lining up your desires with the support of your subconscious, conscious and superconscious. Believing that you cannot be happy and secure until you have financial stability is going about your business backwards. Its efforting in your daily life, while thinking about all you want in your future. Deluding yourself into believing that when you get what you want your life will be more fulfilled. Future wishing and wanting takes you away from the energy and passion that needs to be generated now. When you are congruent on all levels of your being with your desire for prosperity, when you feel as if you already have it—<u>then</u> go out and knock on doors, or make that phone call. Donate that money to charity or give to the homeless <u>before</u> you have all you want–act as if you already are wealthy, and the universe supports you.

Find within how you *want* to feel and know how you *want* to live. <u>Believe</u> that the universe will allow synchronistic events to bring the opportunities to you--and the process is set in motion. Imagine how it would be if you were already living your dream life. Allow yourself to fantasize. Feel it, sense it, taste it as if it's yours—then let it go. Now go about your business doing what you need to do to create your abundance with a lighter heart.

Pretend that you feel secure and are wealthy, and that will produce a feeling in harmony with that reality.

Imagination or reality; your subconscious and the universe don't know the difference. If you need to, "pretend," it will affect your body, both physiologically and emotionally, changing your vibration to bring you what you imagine you already have. Working with magnetic energy is so much easier isn't it, than attempting to "make" it happen. As you imagine what you want as if it is an already "done" deal, the universe responds.

Hidden agendas (combined with beliefs you are not aware of) consistently bring more of what you do not want to experience. Beliefs are part of your habitual thinking, and they cause all sorts of frustration when you don't realize the double messages you're constantly sending out into the universe.

Every time you say a positive affirmation such as. "The universe is providing for all my needs," that little voice inside your head may shout, "that's not true; your wrong!" Even if you're able to change your thoughts, that does not necessarily change your beliefs. Far more than your thoughts, it is your <u>beliefs</u> that are emotionally charged. And the energy of your beliefs will bring about the manifestation of your desires.

If you are not congruent with your desires, your Inner Wisdom working through your emotions, lets you know whenever you are saying one thing yet believing another. The resulting heaviness you may feel, serves as a reminder for you to look at how your contradicting beliefs may be leading to conflict. There's good news, too. Now you know by how you feel what's not working! Your heavy or unpleasant feelings are offering you a choice. You no longer have to continue thinking and believing the same old thing. Instead, you're offered the opportunity to turn your thoughts around as you look out for your best interests.

Your thoughts determine your happiness.

Are you waiting to feel happy until after you've acquired all that you dream of? Does it always seem to be far in your future? If you think about life this way you are probably not much fun to be around. Always waiting for something outside of you to make you happy.

Do you know other people who appear to enjoy themselves and are living happily with less than you have? You always have a choice. You can either create a state of mind that allows you to see and appreciate the pleasure in all you have; or, focus on what you consider is missing in your life. Your thoughts, determined by your beliefs, create this focus. Gratitude brings you what you want, conversely, dissatisfaction brings struggle. You can and do create your own heaven or hell. Your unconditionally loving Inner Guidance allows you complete free will to choose your own path.

Loving your guilt into the light makes way
for abundance to flow.

So often, useless feelings of guilt trigger feelings of not deserving, which can stop you from creating the life you consciously want to have. You feel guilty about not having invited Aunt Maud over for dinner, or for not calling your mother often enough. Maybe you feel that you shouldn't want to be wealthy, or that you can't have everything your heart desires. Just name it: what we do to create feelings of guilt is absolutely endless. Through interaction with my clients and Higher Wisdom, I've come to the conclusion that a person can only feel guilty when they give themselves permission to do so. If you're ready to beat up on yourself for not being "perfect," it usually stems from identifying yourself as an imperfect struggling human. Instead, remember that you are filled with Source energy. When you're not happy with yourself you tend to look for ways to feel less than whole. Feeling guilty is an "acceptable" way to do this. But....it's always uncomfortable. Listen to your beautiful Inner Being that gently tells you—through body language, for example—that guilt is not in your best interest. Guilt keeps you from loving yourself, and throws you out of alignment from your center of peace.

So why hold on to guilt? You may feel badly if you have hurt someone or were deceitful on purpose. Yet, if you are conscious enough to take responsibility, you can probably make amends and release yourself from the situation. Otherwise, why feel guilty at all? Doing anything unintentionally only means that perhaps you did or said something you wish you hadn't. But you can correct it, or apologize, and send love to the other party involved. This is a far more gentle approach than beating up on yourself. You are a work in progress as you recognize that there is always room for improvement. Punishing, guilty thoughts make you feel miserable; forgiving, loving energy allows you to expand your levels of awareness. Know that you do not have to repeat self-defeating patterns of behavior and thought.

You can always change and grow
no matter how old you are.

One of the greatest gifts you can give yourself is to let go of the way you have been. Let go of the way you expect things to be, and imagine that you are ready for a fresh start. Pretend you are an artist with a blank canvas in front of you. At your feet are several pots of paint. Although many of these are the same colors that you have used before, mix them in a different way to create a new style. Let's look first at the Picasso, very bright and abstract. Now, imagine the colors to be subtler with softer hues, and paint a new image of you in line with Cezanne or a Renoir. As the adventurous painter, you can always change the style to suit the new beliefs you would like to adopt. As the harsh painter, you have been your own worst enemy, beating yourself up whenever you didn't live up to your own expectations. Perhaps you're carrying many beliefs that you've accepted as truth about your weaknesses and inadequacies. Now, pick up the brush and create a new you, complete with wonderfully complex stories around your life. As you stop justifying your behavior and thoughts to yourself and others, you'll stop feeling miserable and start feeling wonderful.

HIDDEN AGENDAS STOP YOUR FLOW

When the manifestations that you're working on do not materialize, you can be sure that somewhere you're holding on to a hidden agenda. Its like a thought behind a thought. You may be aware of your conscious thoughts, but unaware of your subconscious or unconscious thoughts. To co-create you need to be in harmony with your desires; essentially, with what you are asking for. So, if you are running up against a brick wall, here are some of the hidden obstacles that might be affecting you.

- Do you have doubts about how much you deserve all you want to have in your life?

- Does what desire make you feel guilty or greedy?
- Do you expect to be able to manifest?
- Will you allow manifestations to come into your life?
- Have you placed conditions (such as a time limit) on receiving what you want?
- Do you stop believing or expecting if your desires do not immediately manifest?
- Are you influenced by negativity from your loved ones, friends, or the media?
- Do you have a subconscious belief that is in conflict with your conscious desire?
- Are you able to surrender your desire to God to allow it to come in its highest form, and without attachment to the outcome?

Many people do not allow themselves to improve their way of life because they hold on to feelings of unworthiness. Are you one of them? Do you have within a critical voice about not deserving, that originally came from an outside source? Do you have a subconscious belief that because your mother was overweight you cannot be thin? It makes no difference when or where these limitations were picked up; its time to let them go.

If you understand and believe that you are filled with Source Energy, how can you not love all of you. You divide yourself into parts that you like, and parts that you don't like. It is impossible to separate Source Energy in that way, for it is unconditional, and is in every fiber of your Being. The only thing playing havoc with your emotions comes from your ego/personality that sits in constant judgment deciding whether you are worthy or not.

Do you feel good inside when you allow thoughts of not deserving to surface, or does it feel unpleasant? Take a second to pretend how you would feel if you were really happy with yourself. Say out loud or silently. "In this now moment, I allow myself to feel worthy and wonderful, filled with the energy of Divine Harmony and Love." As you say this, imagine a feeling of expansion coming over your body, and repeat: "I do deserve to have all I desire, for that is my highest good, and I like the way it feels."

Guilt

This paragraph is for those of you who feel guilty about desiring abundance for yourself. Were you raised with the belief that it is better to give than receive? If you were, a big part was left out. The more you want to give to others, the more you need to give to yourself. Do you really want to be poor because others are poor? If you are poor, how can you financially help others?

The energy of the universe is unlimited, and energy is a form of money, love and joy. If you *really* accept this as a truth, then you also understand how there must be an abundance of everything you have been wanting. Whatever you create for yourself is also available for everyone to create. And, the more you have, the more you can share. Enjoy visualizing how wonderful it will be to help all those people and causes you would like to support. Allow those good feelings to become a part of your life and revel in them.

Expectation

As you send out your energy and visualize what you want, do you *really* expect it to appear in your life? Or, are you instead expending effort but then telling yourself it may not happen? You may not allow yourself to expect success, because you've been disappointed so many times before, and it hurts. Getting your hopes up, doing the work and then being disappointed can be very discouraging and painful. But, let's take a look at the reason "why." In your previous work with visualizations and affirmations, did you qualify your efforts with a "yes, but?" You might have said," I want to win a million dollars on the lottery—but, it probably won't happen." Or, "I want to go on a cruise around the world—but, I don't have that kind of money." How about, "I want to write a best selling novel, or star in a blockbuster movie–but I'm probably not good enough."

This "yes but," syndrome is sending out a vibration of doubt that is canceling out the energy you had set in motion for what you want. You can see that if you want to attract what you choose, it is necessary to release all of that negative energy. You need to create in *harmony* with your Inner Wisdom instead of sending out conflicting energies.

Outside Influences

How much do you listen to the opinions of others, even if they're based on fearful and negative thoughts? It's so easy to buy into all that is "wrong" with the world. If you do so however–if you accept that energy from others–it becomes a part of your energy. And it doesn't feel good. Has living in fear and anxiety ever changed anything in your life in a positive way?

Think about all the predictions for disaster over the years. How much of it has come true? Will you choose fear for your future reality, or would you like to create a more positive experience by changing your focus and your thoughts? Try this: every time you let an outside "authority" negatively affect the way you think, you will feel uncomfortable. If you are in the same room as the source of negativity, cover your solar plexus with your hands. Your solar plexus is where you take in others energy, and if you feel yourself buying into their drama, turn away. Instead, think about how you <u>want</u> to feel. Does buying into their drama help you in any way? You have a choice. Whichever thought you choose, *will* become a part of your life!

Decide to be around uplifting people, those who have a positive outlook on life. Don't listen to, or watch sensational violence or fear based programs on the movies, television, or the radio. Be a guardian of your thoughts and emotions. After all, why would you invite anything in your life that doesn't uplift you and make you feel good?

Allowance

Allowing whatever you are co-creating to come into your life means not demanding that it will come in a certain way, or in the time frame that you want. If you're still placing yourself in the drivers seat with

God in the back seat–if you're complaining that what you are visualizing is not happening fast enough or in the way you want it to, who can you blame but yourself? More than your ego, trust Divine Timing to know whether you're ready to have what you want. The time may be right for the manifestation of your dreams to become reality...then again, maybe not. Its a natural reaction to be impatient. Yet, impatience is a lack of trust in the Divine Order.

As I read for clients I am constantly amazed at how often I see a future situation they have been working on, sitting right in their energy fields. They are not yet aware that anything has happened, as their visualization has not yet gathered enough density to manifest as a reality visible to their outer eyes. If at this point they stop believing that it will happen, (because it has not yet happened) probably <u>nothing will happen.</u> It would be like constantly rewriting the last chapter of a novel. The book never gets finished! To create a finished product you have to write the final chapter and don't give up! Enjoy the time you spend daily co-creating. <u>Trust</u> that the universe is rearranging itself to create what you want, and you'll experience it.

Surrender

One of the hardest and most necessary parts of manifesting is surrender. If you are struggling with this aspect, perhaps the following suggestions will help you. First, visualize and affirm what you want in a way that allows you to feel wonderful. Then, when you have sent out a magnetic energy to attract what you desire, surrender your vision to the universe to come in its highest form. Don't have a fixed idea of how and from where it will come. If you carry the limiting energy of, "It has to be a certain way or else," you are repelling the very thing you want to attract. Attachment to the outcome comes from your ego receiving messages from your subconscious or conscious mind. It's connected with fears, doubts, guilt and anxiety. So, trust is essential. Don't push away the very thing you are so ready to experience. If you feel that you still have an attachment to what you want, imagine that you are putting it in a balloon, which you're holding by the string. Lovingly and with trust, gently let go of the string as you surrender it upwards.

There are so many subtle reasons the manifestation process may not appear to work. If you are not yet manifesting, only you can uncover all your thoughts and fears that are keeping you from succeeding. Take your own inventory of all that you could possibly be thinking and feeling that might be keeping you from your desired outcome.

The stronger and clearer your desire and the more passionate you are, the quicker it will manifest.

Your imagination is your key to creating. The more powerfully you use your imagination to see, feel, and sense what you want to magnetize, the more powerful your ability to magnetize will be. We've seen why it's necessary to be in harmony with your desire to achieve what you want without any contradictory energy. However, there's an exception to this. Sometimes, if a desire is so overwhelmingly strong, it is possible to override the fear that usually cancels out or prolongs the manifestation coming into your life. If you are so determined that nothing can stop you achieving your goal—your probably right!

SUBCONSCIOUS CLUTTER

As you raise your level of awareness and take responsibility for all that is in your experience, you will find this work becomes a natural part of your life.

As you become more aware of your daily thoughts, you'll immediately have the ability to turn them around if you find yourself falling into uncomfortable patterns. You'll notice—and change—patterns of negativity that had been habitual, those from the "before" life that you no longer want.

Your personality/ego is built around beliefs that you tell yourself you need for survival. Your personality decides if you are happy or unhappy. And these decisions are based on beliefs about what you consider to be okay or what is not okay. This ego/personality is a formless part of yourself that runs your life and often creates havoc with your emotions. It is formed from your perception of events in your life based on past experience, and subsequent beliefs. It is not impartial in its view of reality.

Each of us has a different perception of what is real and important in our lives. We each have a different viewpoint about a situation we may have witnessed or experienced, and it's determined by our own frame of reference built from our own experiences. We've all seen, for example, that two children from the same family often have a completely different belief about how they were raised. One child may feel the family was loving and supportive; the other child may

feel they never had enough ι.
remember being miserable. Differeɴ
ferent perspectives. As you change you
change your emotions. With practice, ɩ.
easier and easier.

Your subconscious mind stores informatioɪ
you may not be consciously aware of. These memories
in your subconscious are gathered throughout this lifetime and continue to affect the way you think and
behave in present time. Painful memories are the ones
that tend to create feelings of anger, fear, judgment and
inadequacy: as such, they are very magnetic. These
memories, attached to emotion, are the ones that keep
you from attracting into your life the abundance that
will make your life richer.

So, how do you release any negative programs that
you might hold in your subconscious? How can you
imagine what you want and be completely in harmony
with your desires? Let me show you. Use the various
techniques and affirmations suggested throughout this
book to help you release all that no longer serves you.

Reframing the way you look at your past experiences allows you to see present experiences in a different light. All of the beliefs and expectations that affect
the way you think can be released. Even the fearful,

ones that creep up from your subconscious, giving you all sorts of excuses, can be looked at in the light of new possibilities. Examine old beliefs and ask if they are serving you in a helpful way, or are they instead hindering you. What can you change that will give you a positive outlook to create a positive future?

The beliefs that you hold about how something "should be" determines how you feel. Your reality is simply your perception.

From your experiences you develop a personality you feel justifies who you are. You develop an ego to support and protect your personality as you identify yourself as a certain type. Your ego is typically often angry, fearful, insecure, demanding, greedy and very much into survival. It is the part of you that affects your emotions thereby attracting into your life more lesson and challenges than most of us would like to have. Your ego/personality would have you believe that all pleasure is to be found outside of you. After all, whatever you do not have is the fault of the universe or other people. Very little of it is your fault, is it?

The other part of you, your Inner Guidance, also acts as your intuition. A formless, faceless energy that has a higher vibrational frequency than your ego/personality, it's an aspect of you that's connected to Universal Wisdom. This part is all wise and loving, resonating with joy as it lovingly guides you. Your Inner Wisdom always has a higher perspective of your life than your ego/personality.

Pay attention and you'll realize that your intuition is always guiding you. Recognize, also, those thoughts that are not in harmony with your intuition. Feeling uncomfortable, anxious, sad, angry, or upset is an indicator that you're not in harmony with your Inner Guidance. When you're aware that you don't feel good, always ask yourself what you are thinking about that created these emotions. You will notice that you were focused on something not being the way you wanted it to be. This focus on what you decide is "not right" creates a dissatisfied vibration that acts like a magnet. Everything in your life is a direct result of the energy you have been sending out, so it benefits you in every way to be grateful for what is in your life. What's in your life is a reflection of how you think, both on a conscious and unconscious level. Align your energy with being grateful, and allow your life to be what you want it to be.

Become more conscious of your feelings.

If you have de-sensitized yourself because of too much disappointment and pain in your life, you may not notice whether you're in vibrational harmony with your desires. You may have felt so uncomfortable or numb for so long that it feels like a natural state to be in. You might believe it's normal to feel dejected, bored, angry or sad. Remember: you are always co-creating. If you focus on what is wrong, you give it more energy. Change your focus instead.

Your feelings constantly let you know if you are creating challenges in your life. Check how you feel. Your Inner Guidance always has the highest possible perspective. Therefore, even if you think you know what you want, pay attention to how you feel. If you're uncomfortable as you do your visualizations or affirmations, something is amiss. You may be asking to receive something that is not in your best interest, or you may have a hidden agenda that will not allow you to harmonize with your desire. Or it may simply not be the best time for your manifestation to become a reality.

In today's busy world it is easy to become desensitized to your feelings. We build in excuses, like not having time to meditate, or not being sensitive enough to hear one's intuition. Feeling too busy making a living to support oneself (and perhaps others) doesn't immediately allow time to fine tune your senses. There are lots of reasons, and always excuses. But trying to make things happen is a hard way to go through life. And it's not necessary. You now—and always will—have the option to listen to your wonderful Inner Guidance system. As long as you work on an energy level and pay attention, it will guide you easily and pleasantly twenty-four hours a day, every day.

Take the time to listen to how you feel. The more attuned you become, the easier your life flows. Think about the way you want your life to be and allow powerful and happy feelings to support your vision of the life you're dreaming of. In other words send out a happy trusting vibration as you think about what you want. Become aware of how your body feels. Is your energy expanded and flowing? When you feel a joyful acceptance, and uplifted as you visualize and affirm, you are energetically aligned. And when you send this energy into the universe it will find its equal match. The universe is then rearranging itself around your vibrations, and what you desire will return to you. Now just let go, sit back and trust that it will come in its highest form!

I BELIEVE WHAT?

Our perception of reality is made up of what we <u>believe</u> we hear, think, see and feel. Everything in the universe is just energy that we perceive to be a certain way. We are a bundle of emotions and experiences that are actually reactions based on our subconscious and conscious memories. Very rarely do we see a situation with enough clarity to "see it as it is." Instead we see with reactive eyes, emotions, and biased perceptions. Furthermore, each individual "sees" differently.

Our beliefs about what is right and wrong, about what should or should not be, create havoc with our emotions. Many of our beliefs that served us in the past are actually creating limitations in our lives today. For instance, we believe that we need to think and act a certain way to be "spiritual." Yet we all have different beliefs about what that means.

I have questioned my spiritual commitment. Somewhere in my psyche I had decided that I didn't spend enough time in meditation each day. So what is enough and how did it make me feel to think that I wasn't spiritual enough? Well, I got to beat myself up, and make excuses about why I wasn't ready to let go of behaviors and thoughts that were not "spiritual" enough. I felt uncomfortable. Yet at the same time, as I connected with my Inner Wisdom, I realized there was nothing I could do that was *not* spiritual. I *am* a being of Spirit. The whole essence of who I am is spiritual. However, my judgments and beliefs about what was spiritual and more importantly what was *not* were negatively affecting me–until I reframed my thinking.

We accept others ideas, especially parents, teachers, churches and gurus about what makes us 'okay' or not 'okay.' Whenever we do this, we give away our power, either to a force or to a person, and we decide that they are wiser or more conscious than we are. This leaves us not feeling very good inside. We are also left feeling dependent on making sure we get into the good graces of those who we have decided will judge us. Let go of the idea that you are less than a Spiritual Being, and allow yourself one less burdensome belief to carry. Relax, and begin to enjoy a sense of freedom.

Circumstances and events in your life reflect back to you a pattern of thought. Look at where and how you'd like things to be different, and intentionally create it. If don't feel good about yourself, if you believe that you're inferior or a "loser," then you'll probably find yourself mixing with those who share similar feelings. Your life will mirror back to you a picture that reinforces your belief systems. To change your life, look at the belief that created a certain situation. Change that core belief so that you may alter the outcome to something you desire. This assures that you don't repeat the same negative, painful and depressing scenario again. What you give, you receive. Conflicting beliefs will negatively affect your process of creating.

You attract the compliment for whatever is within you that needs healing.

When what you are co-creating doesn't materialize in your time frame, understand the relevance of Divine Timing. Source doesn't make mistakes, so ask yourself. "Does what I want infringe on anybody else, or am I interfering with someone's choice in life? It's also quite possible that the timing may not be right. Or perhaps you are including someone else in your manifesting process that may not be in harmony with your vision. Whatever the reason, trust that right now in your frustration, you are being given the opportunity to grow emotionally and spiritually. It may simply be that you need more time to become compatible with what you desire. Ask yourself if you are really ready for all that you want. For example, sometimes we want to become a CEO without having gained the knowledge and experience we would have acquired by working our way from the bottom of a company to the top. The larger picture allows us to see how important it is to get there at the right time: otherwise, we may miss parts of the puzzle that allow us to become more whole and connected with our highest wisdom, as we follow our soul's plan.

NOT SO HIDDEN AGENDAS

In my experience, I've found that if I really want something—as I imagine, affirm, and visualize it—and I don't get that wonderful high flowing energy filling my body, I need to pay attention. Many times I would press on, imagining and visualizing what I wanted but ignoring that little nagging feeling inside. Without fail, when you do not pay attention to your Inner Guidance, you will probably not manifest what you want. Or, your manifestation will not bring you the satisfaction that you were looking for.

In the long run, it's not going to work. If you don't listen to your intuition, if you don't heed this Inner Guidance system, you are still trying to control your life from your personality, and "make" it happen. You're setting yourself up to learn a lesson. Trust your

Inner Wisdom. Visualize, affirm, feel with intensity, and surrender it to the Highest Power. Or, perhaps you enjoy doing things the hard way and thrive on struggle. Which ever way you choose, know that you have a choice!

Another "not so hidden" agenda is knowing that you want to change but feeling powerless to do so. You find yourself in an overwhelming place of fear, sadness or inertia where you cannot muster enough energy to even imagine what you want. The best of us sometimes experience that funk, when it seems that nothing helps.

If you find yourself in one of these moods, and you've tried everything—playing your favorite music, watching a funny movie, meditating or working out at the gym—yet you still feel like playing the victim, I only have one suggestion: climb into bed and pull the covers over you head and decide to start fresh in the morning. Don't judge yourself for being this way, just look at it as temporary behavior. Know that little by little, as you become aware that you are always creating something, you will find the energy to pay attention to your thoughts. The unpleasant idea that you are creating more of what you do not want will eventually allow you to change your thought pattern. Only you think your thoughts; only you can change them.

As you hide under the covers, find a memory of a time when you felt good and go back to that time in your imagination. Perhaps you were laughing or being silly with a friend, brother, or sister. Or you were enjoying watching a puppy or kitten play. Many of us can find pleasure in watching a young child giggle with delight looking at an ant hurriedly move about, or a bird fly overhead. Do you have a favorite place, or a special gift from a friend? Find that special place or memory that has good feelings connected to it. Notice in your mind's eye as much of the surroundings in as great a detail as you can. Then, send out your affirmations:

"Universe, in this moment I am ready to feel uplifted. I want this feeling to become stronger and stronger as I remember how I feel when I'm happy and content." As you say these words, begin to be aware of a slight change in your mood. Continue imagining it, letting it become your reality. As you let the feeling grow stronger and stronger, tell the universe: "As I let my body and emotions begin to vibrate at a higher, finer frequency I am feeling better and better. And I open to let this good feeling become a part of my everyday life. I am beginning to feel more powerful. As I do this, I know that I am ready to let happiness and joy become a part of my life."

Once you are feeling better (even if still in bed,) imagine what you want to attract into your life. Remember that what you are asking for already exists on a subatomic particle level. All you have to do is match your energy to the energy of what you want to have. That means affirming and visualizing from a place of feeling good and lighthearted, knowing its yours for the asking, not from a place of need.

Begin turning your life around now. Let what you don't want create an energy inside you. Use this energy to inspire yourself to dream about what you do want. Let your dreams, empowered with passion and intensity, become a reality.

Chapter Three

ATTRACTING LOVE

Are you ready to meet that special person with whom you'll share your life as a soulmate? Have you been wondering how to find someone to love? Are you perplexed as to how to attract the love of your life? If any of this applies to you, take hope. Various steps, when practiced, will enable you to fine tune your magnetic vibration and attract your perfect mate.

Perhaps you have romantic dreams of being loved and cherished. You may daydream away hours fantasizing about how it would feel to be loved and nurtured for the rest of your life. Or you may imagine that finding your soulmate will mean sharing a love that knows no barriers of time and space, has no bounds or limitations. Perhaps you dream this love has even followed you through many lifetimes. Generally speaking, unless you have lost faith through too many previous unfulfilling or even tragic relationships, you carry within your heart the eternal hope—if not the belief—that this type of love exists. But you don't know where to go to meet that special someone.

So, if you're lonely or sad, perhaps even feeling in despair that you may never meet your soulmate, regain your faith. First of all there is not just one, but *many* soulmates out there with whom you can connect. And the good news is, that once you know this, you don't even have to search to find your loved one! Learn how to match frequencies with a soulmate and the universe will automatically arrange that you *will* meet each other. Sometime, somewhere, you will both be destined to make this connection and definitely continue on your journey together.

IF LOVE ALREADY EXISTS, WHY DON'T I HAVE IT?

Deep inside most of us, we feel incomplete. We often feel that "something's missing." Two of the reasons explained to me by my Inner Guidance are as follows: An incomplete sense of self stems from our subconscious, conscious, and superconscious not being aligned and in harmony with each other. And, also from a feeling that we are separate from Source Energy. It really isn't surprising, for we tend to spend most of our time focused on the physical aspects of our daily life, instead of what needs to be our primary focus: the inner part of ourselves. As a result, we spend a lot of our time judging and criticizing people and events, and usually ending up feeling very un-spiritual in our behavior. Filled with fear, many of us might even feel that Source exists outside or apart from ourselves and simply presides over us in judgment like a wrathful parent. As we continue to search for our soulmate, we know unconsciously, deep within our being, that love is the vibration of oneness. We yearn to reconnect and once more know this experience. When we don't immediately find it, our search to rekindle that wonderful feeling spurs us on. Yet, so often our focus is on finding this wholeness outside of us, instead of within.

When we first fall in love, we are in love with life, and for a while we are in love with love. In this intense emotional state, we are vibrating at a high frequency. In this state of happiness and enthusiasm it's easy to connect with our Source Energy. After experiencing this feeling which is so enticing and exhilarating, we find ourselves in a constant search for it. We expect and hope to capture that feeling over and over through our lover or lovers. Ultimately it is this unity and love with another which can lead us to a higher and greater understanding of the love of self and Source. So it is in reality, no great wonder that we yearn to connect with someone who is our compliment.

Your soul knows your life purpose.

As we spend most of our everyday lives forgetting that we are spiritual beings having an earthly experience, our Inner Wisdom offers us the chance to use each relationship we find ourselves in to further our growth, and open our hearts.

My Inner Guidance has imparted many wonderful dialogues to me centered around this subject, and has also expanded my views about Love, Soul Psychology, Soulmates and Magnetic Attraction. Through their loving thoughts, they have given me an overview of life and love that has helped me to understand the perfection of each and every relationship that we as human beings attract into our lives. And in my own personal experience, the various individuals who have come to me from all walks of life have also demonstrated time and time again this very same theme. That indeed there is a thread that runs throughout time and space which connects us all soul to soul.

OUR RELATIONSHIPS ARE
ALWAYS PERFECT

Many people I meet are not aware that the relationship they are experiencing in the present is perfect for them, at this moment. We hold so many beliefs about what a perfect relationship is. Beliefs about how our lover or friends should act, think or feel. If they don't live up to our expectations, we may simply convince ourselves that we are in the "wrong" relationship. We may tell ourselves that we are unloved or unappreciated in some way. Or we may simply say that we are still in the process of searching for the "right" one.

If you're feeling this way–stop, and take a look at your thoughts. If you can't seem to attract a loving, supportive relationship into your life, or you are not happy with aspects of your current relationship, it's a signal to look within. Start by asking yourself some questions.

- How loving are you to yourself?
- Do you *really* feel that you deserve to be loved?
- Do you have a belief that you are unlovable or not really capable of loving another without conditions? If you're pointing the finger at your lover, perhaps you should ask yourself why you've chosen to be with this partner in the first place?

Be assured of this: in this moment, you're in this particular relationship because you and your partner are both vibrating at a similar frequency. Serving as a perfect mirror, your partner is showing you a part of yourself that needs healing. Through the presence of this partner, he/ she is offering you the chance to look deeply within to see where you don't feel whole. Or, where you're in pain or detached, or possibly protecting yourself from more heartache.

Your relationships serve you by allowing for inner reflection, giving you the opportunity to transform problems into growth. With this higher perspective, there is no longer any need to focus on the disappointments of a relationship. Simply create a relationship with yourself that is more loving and open. The rest will follow. With this expanded vision, you'll no longer feel like a victim. Instead, you'll transform the belief of "nobody loves me" into the more positive, "I am lovable, and I am ready to attract love into my life!"

Whatever you are experiencing is directly related to the thoughts and feelings you are having about yourself and those around you.

Learn how to consciously use your magnetic emotions to create your life in a way that brings you harmony. Let's say your spouse, friend or child indulges in self-destructive behavior, such as drugs, overeating or excessive drinking. The worst reaction is also the most natural one, that of focusing on the problem. Remember: whatever you focus on will become stronger as the universe responds to your energy. So by focusing on what you see as "wrong," you will actually be reinforcing the behavior. The energy of your thoughts about the behavior is unconsciously picked up by the other person involved and reinforces the addiction. Help to reinforce change by focusing on your loved one's wholeness, by imagining them feeling healthy and happy and not needing to abuse themselves in any way. The magnetic energy that you broadcast will unconsciously affect their energy field. And you've helped to support a behavior change.

Do you have anyone in your life who is continually letting you down by betraying you, or acting in an unloving manner? If so, watch your reactions. Notice what thoughts you're sending in their direction. There's a good chance you're struggling with them in your mind as well as on a physical level. As humans, we have a natural tendency to focus on how bad things are. So, if you are focusing on what's wrong, don't berate yourself for reacting negatively. Simply understand that by your choice of focus you are reinforcing more of the same behavior.

The more you understand this concept, the quicker you will become adept at changing your thoughts. Imagining positive situations will reinforce positive changes in behavior, it is the most loving way to help those you care about.

Whatever path you have chosen, in each new moment
you are offered the chance to start fresh with an
awakened understanding.

Let's take Joe, for example. In his session, he wanted to focus on why he couldn't find a girlfriend who
loved him enough to marry him. He attracted women
who seemed to match him perfectly. Yet, when Joe
became serious about a relationship, his partner would
vanish. Tuning into Joe from a higher level, I could see
psychically that Joe adored his mother, he was the apple
of her eye. His mother was on a pedestal; unconsciously he was comparing all of his girlfriends to her. Joe was
consciously affirming that he was ready to be married;
yet it remained a complete puzzle to him as to why no
one else could see what a good husband he would be.
Unconsciously, he was sending out vibrations into the
universe that were counteracting his desire for a loving
partner. According to Joe, he didn't want to marry
someone who would mother him. Yet his thoughts were
different: "She isn't as caring as my mother." Or: "If she
really loved me she would cater to my needs." His belief
was that his girlfriend didn't love him as much as his
mother did. That negative vibration created resulting
vibrations from Joe's girlfriend to support this premise.
In essence, Joe created the situation by questioning how
much she loved him compared to his mother.

The two opposing vibrations he was emitting, "I want love," and "You don't love me enough," were canceling each other out, creating a seeming mismatch of energies. In fact, he was receiving *exactly* what he was sending out to the universe. Joe's girlfriend joined him in feeling that her love for him was being rejected. She, too, doubted Joe's love for her.

When his conscious and unconscious thought patterns were pointed out to him, Joe was absolutely amazed that he was pushing away the very thing he desired. He became more aware of his hidden beliefs about how a lover should think and act, and was able to let go of his limiting ideas about comparisons being important. He is now dating a delightful lady, and they seem to be very loving and open couple together. Now that Joe's vibration is in alignment with his desire for a healthy relationship, he will probably find it in his current one. Even if this relationship does not lead to marriage, Joe now understands that he has progressed one step further. This present situation is offering him exactly what he needs right now for his own understanding and awakening.

Thinking back on your relationships, it may appear that you have made choices from an unconscious level, almost from an intuitive place that you may not always have consciously understood. Remember, that your soul, (even if it's not heard on a conscious level) is always guiding you towards your next partner or friend for your growth. Take responsibility for whom you attract, and understand that relationships are in our lives for a purpose. Unless you do so, you may search tirelessly, always looking for the "right" person to love. When you don't seem to find the "right" one, it is not necessarily because you're looking in the wrong place. Don't let yourself become confused. While you may ultimately be looking for the "perfect" partner, at that precise moment you are already with the right partner for your immediate needs.

You might want to understand why you've created certain experiences with your loved ones. Why relationships often end so differently than what "might have been." Having insight to the larger picture allows you to rise above the feeling that somehow you failed, or conversely that it was all the other persons fault. Your soul is always guiding you towards perfect opportunities for growth. Yet we don't always have a clear connection with our Inner Wisdom to receive this higher perspective. Indeed, if we don't have an overview we sometimes miss what is being offered to us. Consequently, we may find frustration and blame filling our lives. The strength and pull of our ego without the higher perspective makes sure that we listen to our emotional body reactions, which tend to keep us repeating the same old patterns.

When you make decisions about whom you choose to be with, remember that you are constantly sending out vibrations with every powerful thought you have. Whomever you attract into your life reflects an aspect of who you are. This perfect mirror in the form of an event or personality shows how you truly think and believe in any given moment.

Joan is a perfect example. I can hear and see the horror on her face as she told me how, before she made her decision to get married, it was agreed that the one thing she could not tolerate was infidelity . She was utterly focused on this *not* happening in her marriage. It almost destroyed Joan to find out how many affairs her husband had experienced over the ten years of their marriage.

Joan felt like a victim, and could not believe that her worst fears had come true. Ironically, by focusing so much energy upon what she did *not* want in her marriage, she had unconsciously sent out a message that worked against her and became one of life's lessons. Joan failed to remember that the universe does not understand the phrase "don't want." The energy connected with her thoughts and emotions gave her exactly what she focused upon.

As the initial damage had been done, Joan had the choice of choosing awareness or anger and limitation. If she continued to imagine her husband indulging in his infidelity, always expecting the worst, she would definitely be reinforcing this kind of behavior. To help him change she needed to see him feeling loving towards her and feeling good about himself. She needed to picture him in his wholeness, strong and focused on holding his marriage together.

Whether Joan decided to stay with her husband or not, it would be important for her to see that she was not a victim. She also needed to understand that her fear of this type of behavior helped to create it in the first place by the law of cause and effect. I believe they were both playing out roles that balanced their past life karma together as well. Painful as their relationship was, I tried to help Joan to understand that it was exactly what she needed. Her husband's infidelity allowed her to see how negative thinking and fear had attracted the very situation that she was so against. Remember that the more you focus on a situation, the more you get it!

LOOKING IN THE MIRROR OF LIFE

Think of the outside world and everyone in it as a reflection of your inner world. Play with the idea that all the personalities in your life are reflecting back aspects of you. Some people are loving and joyful. It's usually easy to claim that loving part inside of you. Other people may be grumpy, mean or miserable. It's not so easy to acknowledge that you may have those less than loving qualities residing somewhere inside you, is it? But you do. We all do. Look deeply enough and you'll recognize that all of your outside experiences resonate with inward perspectives.

Each relationship you attract into your life will mirror back to you exactly what you need for new insight. Your level of awareness determines which lessons and growth you are next ready to experience. Accept this, and your degree of readiness will bring love into your life. A love who will either mirror back to you your weaknesses, insecurity and fears, or facilitate your growth through joy as you become stronger and more centered. Your consciousness determines whether you learn and grow through struggle and pain, or joyful experiences.

For example, if you are experiencing an abusive relationship perhaps you will learn why you're in it. Turn inward and take notice of how much–or how little—self-love you have. A natural reaction is to blame the other party. But if you're feeling this way, stop right now and take a deep breath. Has blame given you peace of mind? It's *not* empowering is it? As you look back at your life, perhaps you'll even see that you have a pattern of attracting this type of relationship over and over again. Of one thing you can be almost certain: unless you look at your relationship differently, this type of person is not going to go away. This individual is in your life because of your invitation! Something inside of you has attracted a relationship with one who does not respect or appreciate your way of being. Perhaps this person doesn't allow you to be your true self. Maybe he or she wants you to be a certain way that's different than who you really are. If this is true, again, it's time to look in the mirror. Take responsibility for your part in the relationship.

If you find yourself complaining that your lover or friend doesn't respect you, ask yourself some simple questions.

- How much respect do you feel towards yourself?
- Do you *really* listen to your needs?

- Do you truly appreciate yourself or are you your own worst enemy? Perhaps you complain that your partner doesn't love you enough. If that's the case, turn it around and ask yourself how much do you love yourself?
- Do you constantly criticize yourself?
- Do you respect others, or do you feel that you have all the answers?
- Do you think other people know as much about life as you do?

Become more in touch with yourself in situations where you point the finger at someone else and say, "you shouldn't be that way!" Every time you find yourself placing blame on someone else, turn it around and question your motivation. Replace the "you" with "I". Examine your own beliefs and expectations. How you feel. Your emotions will let you know if what you are creating is in harmony with your Inner Wisdom, or if you are out of harmony and are creating what you do not want.

Whomever you attract into your life at any given time is exactly right for you.

Your companions are with you in response to your vibrational output. Whatever energy you're emitting is met with its equal match. For example: if you feel insecure, you may attract someone to further bring out your insecurities. Or conversely, you may attract a positive balance and find someone that supports you with so much love that you become more secure within yourself.

The person who feels insecure may feel incapable of loving or being loved. That flow of energy will most likely find someone who will act as a mirror and trigger the negative feelings. Instead, focus on being loving and gentle and non-judgmental of your feelings of insecurity. Attract a balanced supportive relationship with one who will bring out your strengths.

Co-creating your life in harmony with your Inner Wisdom requires that you look deeply within. Become sensitive to your intuitive responses. Left to your own devices, you may decide that there are areas within that are best left alone. Or, you might decide that the debris could be swept under the rug to stay there for as long as you choose to not clean house. However, this "blind eye" syndrome is not beneficial to you. Ultimately it will cause other people to come into your life to act as facilitators. Facilitators—or primary relationships—help you to learn and master the greatest lessons needed in order to achieve wholeness in this lifetime. You are never without teachers. And your greatest teacher of all is within and has a direct pipeline to access the highest wisdom imaginable–Source. As a live in mentor, your Inner Guidance creates situations and experiences that you need for inner growth. Relationships will act as the mirror you need to reflect back places within that could use a little housecleaning.

Maria is an example of how our thoughts and beliefs mirror that which we carry within, both subconsciously and consciously. When she arrived for her appointment it was obvious that she had been crying. She carried in her aura a very dark energy of depression although she was one of the gentlest and most thoughtful people you could ever hope to meet. Her husband was seemingly the opposite of Maria. He was abusive mentally and physically, especially when he was drinking heavily. Maria was a nurse, a mother and a wife. She gave to others all day long, and truly was a "Florence Nightingale." So to say Maria's life mirrored what she needed would not seem to make sense. Giving Maria a psychic reading, I could see that, as a child, her father had abused her. Her brothers had also abused her. Maria had forgiven them and did not harbor inner hostility. She certainly didn't deserve this kind of life. And yet this was her reality.

What was Maria's lesson? Why was she was surrounded by abusive people? Through her past experiences she had acquired low self-esteem. In Maria's mind she was worthless and unlovable, and her sub-conscious memories created a mirror for her to look within. When she realized that she didn't really love herself, she understood why she was married to a brutish man who did not return her affections. Maria and her husband also had past life karma together. But, because Maria took abuse in this life without being vindictive towards those who dealt it out, she released herself from creating any new negative karma with them.

Maria's job then became one of finding love in her heart for herself. Maria always found it easier to see the best in everyone else before seeing it in herself. Recognizing that Source is within everyone, including her own being, Maria realized that she deserves to receive just as much love as she gives to others. With new understanding Maria will be able to bring into her life the kind of warmth and love that she is ready to receive. She may have to leave her husband to make room for this to occur, however. It is possible, but not likely, that her husband will change. Regardless, Maria will do what is best for her now that she knows she "deserves" more.

Some of you might recognize yourself in Maria's story. If you look in a mirror at yourself, do you see a beautiful Being of Light, a child of God? Do you recognize that Being as you? Are you able to see your highest potential? Do you see who you are beyond the solid form of your reflection? How painful and depressing it would be to look in your mirror and have an image reflected back to you that doesn't even like you! Don't let your mirror image focus on what is "wrong" with you?

Rejection of Self will most definitely find a reflection that attracts negative relationships into your life.

Use this understanding to find your strengths and inner beauty. As a result, you will become more secure within yourself about your gifts, abilities, and personal spiritual growth. Remind yourself: you are not your accomplishments or outer beauty as these are just physical aspects. Remember, first and foremost you are a spiritual being connected to Source, perfect in your seeming imperfection as you journey into wholeness.

Some of you may find it difficult not to focus on what you consider to be wrong with you. This can become a habitual way of thinking. Yet, if you are not happy with the way your life is going you *do* have a choice. Only you think your thoughts. Although it takes some work to reframe the way you think about yourself and life, it is easily done if you listen to your feelings.

93

Nobody outside of you can do this process for you. If you are not sure in what direction your thoughts are leading you, take a look around. Your outer life is always a reflection of what is going on inside, even if you would like to think differently.

Look at your friends and the people with whom you interact throughout your day. Do you find that you often surround yourself with those who think and act the same as you? It makes sense. The similarities give you a feeling of familiarity and comfort, instead of feelings of confrontation or discomfort that sometimes occur when you're among people who have a different standard of morals and ethics than your own.

However, you may be the type of person who has consciously or unconsciously bought into the myth of "no pain no gain." Accepted as fact, you may believe on some level that you accelerate your growth when you're experiencing painful situations. Because of that underlying belief, you will tend to attract people into your life who have a different set of values than yours. You may unconsciously invite these relationships into your life believing that confrontation may trigger inner change.

Forcing inner changes will usually create disharmony and confrontation. At the very least, it will result in a challenging relationship that feels similar to being on a roller coaster. You may be propelled into growth by your need to survive, but do you really want to do it this way if you have a choice? If you fit into this pattern and are ready for transformation, decide you will send a different energy out into the universe. Believe and expect that you are ready for growth through pleasurable experiences!

Sometimes those who think and act differently from us reflect back those parts within ourselves that we fear, or have swept under the rug. Perhaps their purpose is to show you where you're blocked creatively. Maybe hidden emotions need to be addressed. Conflict usually reflects back something about ourselves that we do not like nor want to acknowledge. I am constantly being shown where I hold on to beliefs about how I expect friends to behave. For example: If I'm feeling frustrated and disappointed by someone else's thoughtlessness, I choose to let go of the idea of how people in my life should act and think. As a result, I'm free of expectation, and don't create a negative energy around the situation. I realize that my choice of thoughts about the situation will either give me an unpleasant or happy experience, its up to me to determine the outcome.

Circumstances that we find ourselves in continuously reflect back our patterns of thoughts, either conscious or unconscious. As you look at your life, where and how would you like things to be different? To change your life, look at the beliefs you hold onto that create certain situations. Change these core beliefs if necessary, so that you may alter the outcome to something you desire. This assures that you do not repeat the same negative, painful and depressing scenario again. What we give to life, we receive back. So if you want more love, give more love. It may be that you need to be more generous to others instead of primarily thinking about yourself.

Be aware throughout your day of how you react to those around you. Repeatedly, you may find yourself in a constant state of judging others, either approving or disapproving of their behavior or their appearance. It often seems that the people closest to us are the ones who push our buttons most easily. In a second, our loved ones can trigger feelings of anger, sadness, frustration, and yes, even happiness. If you truly want to become more loving, realize that those with whom you interact are triggering your self-reflection. You may see in your companion something about yourself that you love and are happy with. Or, you may notice things that you don't like, things you may have hidden away within yourself and haven't yet acknowledged. Look at whom you've invited into your life to tell you how you feel about yourself. After all, your outer life is simply a manifested reflection of your inner beliefs.

You attract the compliment for whatever is within you that needs healing.

You might be in a situation like Maria's where it's difficult to understand why you're being treated in a mean, deceitful or critical fashion. Take a look inside to see if you can discover what lies buried within. If someone is being mean, look at where you might be mean and unloving if not to others, then to yourself. Your guidance will consistently send you these situations until you realize you can change. The outer world always reflects the inner world, even if the inner world is hidden deep within.

The relationship between James and Dawn reflected one of the clearest mirrors I'd ever seen between two people. I had known and worked with Dawn for quite a few years. She had always been heterosexual in her relationships until she found a woman with whom she fell deeply in love. It was as much as a surprise to her as to anyone else who knew her. The relationship was solid and lasted a couple of years. Whenever I gave her a reading during that time, I could distinctly see her happily married in a heterosexual relationship with a family of her own. A few years later, as her gay relationship was coming to an end, Dawn again talked about how ready she was to find a man to love and be loved by.

A few months later Dawn met James. She was very attracted to him, but found him to be somewhat unusual. James liked to appear in public dressed up in women's clothing. She assured me he was heterosexual but was quite comfortable with cross-dressing. Looking at their energy together, it was absolutely amazing how perfectly matched they were. James was bringing out Dawn's female qualities. In turn, she was supporting his acceptance of himself exactly as he was. By accepting his behavior as okay, Dawn was, in fact, reinforcing his masculine strengths.

They did not meet simply by chance. It was absolutely divinely choreographed for them to come together. Their energies together, a combination of masculine and feminine, served as perfect mirrors for both of them to look deeply within and find their wholeness. Whatever the outcome, both Dawn and James received exactly what they needed at the time.

Viewing life from a higher perspective, allows you to see that life is perfect in its seeming imperfection. Look without judgment and preconceived beliefs about how life should be to benefit from all that you encounter.

An exercise that helps me utilize my experiences in a positive way involves looking at the people who trigger within me the most judgment. Realizing what it is about them that I find upsetting, I search my own personality for that same quality within myself, however small. Reviewing from a place of non-judgment allows me to become more aware of areas within myself that still need healing. Areas, that when healed, will bring me closer to my wholeness.

Love and understanding are the greatest therapies.
Self-love allows you to be centered, not selfish.

You may agree that the definition of a selfless love is giving to others before you give to yourself. But look at how much you need those others to express their gratefulness to you. How often do you simply give for the sake of giving without needing acknowledgment? If you're honest, you might realize that you are expecting something back. Often, wanting to receive appreciation or love is one of the only ways you're aware of to reinforce that you are really lovable and worthy. And so you give to receive. If this applies to you, the energy vibration you are sending out is one that says; "I don't feel good enough, I don't think I'm wonderful, so please tell me how thoughtful and nice I am."

Because of this flow of insecure energy, you may receive negative reactions from others. You might feel taken advantage of, or not appreciated. In addition, if you lack in self-love yet keep giving to others, the well will soon run dry and you will become depleted. And if your well is empty, how much can you get out of it? Take care of yourself by recognizing the Source within all mankind, including yourself. Your well will be full, and you will have plenty to share.

It feels so wonderful to give yourself enough time to enjoy the things that make you feel good. So take time to indulge, whether it's by having a massage, going to the gym, or taking a bubble bath surrounded by scented candles. Renew yourself with quiet time, meditation and by communing with nature. The more you give to yourself, the more you have to give to others. The happier you are, the more magnetic you become. And the more able you'll be to attract abundance into your life so that you may share it with others.

Each and every person that you choose to be
with will offer you exactly what you
need at that time in your life.

Perhaps as you evaluate your present relationships you may gain a new perspective, one that gives you a greater understanding of what opportunities you are receiving for your spiritual growth. See what you are reflecting back to each other. Notice how this relationship is giving you the chance to peel off more emotional layers of negativity, doubt, fear and lack of trust.

You may feel that the relationship you are in right now is not exactly what you want. But be assured that until you are ready to make conscious decisions and shifts, it is exactly what you need. And as you work with your emotions and lighten your vibration, you become closer in vibrational harmony with your Inner Wisdom.

KARMA AND REINCARNATION

"I feel like I've known you before." How many times have you said or thought this after meeting someone new, feeling a strong connection or sense of familiarity with them? Reincarnation will be familiar to some of you. Others may not know enough about it to believe or not believe. Some of you may not allow this concept to even be a possibility. Whatever your beliefs, it does not affect in any way your power of magnetic attraction and your ability to manifest.

To reincarnate means having lived more than one lifetime on earth in different bodies, and having had different lifetimes of experience. As the same soul or Divine Spark, you incarnate into different physical bodies in different time periods. Choosing to do this to express your Divine Energy in the physical, you may be rich or poor, male or female. You may choose to complete lessons by returning with the same group of people you have experienced other lifetimes with. Whatever growth you need, you will place yourself in the most opportune environment to accomplish your goals. You may choose a life where you go to college in New York instead of learning on the plains of Africa. Everyone is a different warehouse of energy and each of us carries within a unique persona at different stages of consciousness.

Reincarnation offers you the chance to create your own destiny as you pass through many stages of awareness. Until you reach a more aware state of consciousness, you may feel that you are not in control of your life. Yet, within certain parameters that you set up for yourself before incarnating, know that you have complete free will. You can choose to make the best of the situations you find yourself in, or give up, and feel helpless. Once you're here, your choice of situations and people to be experienced are your karmic responsibilities.

Karma is like cause and effect, and it's accumulated over many lifetimes. Every action creates a reaction. It explains why you sometimes see a wonderful person having such a difficult life, and someone else who is mean and dishonest seemingly enjoying an easy life. In order to understand it, you may need to accept that the wonderful person may be paying off a karmic debt for "deeds done" in a past lifetime, or vice versa. Your life and all the events in it are leading you on a journey towards wholeness, where eventually you are able to transcend your karma. Although various events andrelationships in this life are predestined, what you do with these experiences is up to you. We always have the option to use everything that comes our way as a tool to further our growth and awareness. Soon we begin to see that effect creates cause, as we master the art of co-creating. At this point in our lives, we begin to really work in harmony with all we have chosen to experience.

How might you overcome karmic situations that seem to be negative? here's an example: A handsome young man, Garrett loved to play sports, and party.

He exuded vitality and had so many interests that he could barely find enough hours in the day. One night after a late party he was in a bad car accident. Garrett woke up paralyzed from the waist down. You can imagine his ensuing state of depression.

He spent the next year in bed with no desire to do anything, not even to live. A group of friends bought him a special wheelchair, one that he could use in wheelchair marathons. Garrett was encouraged to try it out, and gradually began to find some interest in life again. Another year went by, and Garrett has now won so many marathons that he has earned enough money to buy a house. He is an absolute inspiration to those around him and has enough enthusiasm for two people.

Something as serious as Garrett's accident is usually a predestined karmic choice. There would have been virtually no way he could have avoided it. How he responded to his situation was absolutely his choice, however. Garrett had complete free will. He could have chosen to either stay in his victim role or uovercome his challenging situation and become an inspiration to others. Garrett chose to evolve and follow his highest soul path in this lifetime.

Life is continuous. We are all made up of particles of energy. Since energy never dies, it becomes imposible for us to die as the essence of our being continues to evolve. It is as if we simply drop our outer form once it has served its purpose and pick a different costume to play a different role the next time around. Once we incarnate into this lifetime, it is up to each of us as to how conscious we become. Its up to each one of us to decide how we utilize our capabilities, and to what degree we choose to recognize the choices and opportunities available.

As you entered into your physical body you took on a heaviness in your vibration, and lost your conscious connection with these higher aspects of yourself. This lack of communication with your Inner Wisdom created within you the need to "do it yourself." Consequently, you created a lot of struggle and suffering as you learned that doing it your way was not necessarily the easiest and most expeditious.

You may or may not believe in past lives. Or, you might be making way for reincarnation to become a possibility. It doesn't matter because your soul already knows. Your soul, made up of Source Energy, is your lifeline to Source. And your soul contains all the experiences you have had throughout your many lifetimes.

All of our souls are at a different stages of growth. Our soul "knows" what is best for us as it offers us great wisdom and guidance, allowing us to grow and develop in accordance with the "bigger picture." Our personalities only think and believe they know. When you meet someone you feel you've known before, recognize that you are aspects of the same soul family. Know, too, that although another soul may feel familiar, most of us are completely unaware of why we have come together again in this life. We are not consciously aware of our prior programming that ties us, yet we feel the connection.

Having chosen to experience life in this body, all of your reasons for being born are stored within. As your path unfolds, you will attract the experiences you need to balance your karma and to transcend obstacles. As you exercise your free will in attracting experiences, life becomes a wonderfully exciting adventure. You have the ability to create your life by your conscious thoughts, all for your own growth. Everything that's in your life, you have created for a reason.

If you want to experience something different,
you have the power to change your thoughts
and to deliberately co-create whatever
your heart desires.

When it is suggested that we are responsible for our life and all that is in it, many people immediately deny it: "No way would I have chosen this life for myself!" Quite often, this vehement response is the fallout from a relationship with parents or a spouse. In my practice, I have found that as the role of karma is explained and understood, most people come to realize why they have placed themselves in challenging situations with various people in their lives. For as you gain another perspective, the pieces of the puzzle begin to fit together.

SOUL REUNIONS

In each lifetime, we usually have no conscious memory of past life experiences. This is a choice of our soul. After all we have a challenging enough time working with our lives right here and now ! Experiencing through new eyes in this now moment offers a fresh approach. Not one that is clouded or colored by past emotions. But when we meet someone and have a soul to soul connection, the attraction will still be there.

Our soul is always guiding us thorough our intuition as we journey through life, yet we so often pay no heed. We believe that we know what is best for us based not necessarily on our deeper truths, but on what we pick up from our ego/personality, family, friends, teachers and the media.

Every lifetime that we share with someone, whether it's a love or hate relationship, is recorded within our soul. That soul record is the reason we are able to meet someone and feel an immediate connection, be it one of attraction or repulsion. Our souls continue to connect again and again as we return in different bodies. Only the costumes are different. We meet up with familiar souls wearing different personalities or hats. We meet up with similar themes, but in situations that offer us a variety of opportunities to play out our unfolding dramas. Each of us has a myriad of invisible karmic ribbons connecting us with our soul family. This link with our soul family is connected with the past lives we have experienced together and is carried within us in our unconscious cellular memory into this lifetime.

The people with whom you choose to be connected have usually been with you through many lifetimes.

Do you find yourself making excuses for the way you are, blaming your childhood or past relationships? Your past experiences with family, friends and lovers, in this life as well as past lives are all exactly as they are meant to be. Although your personality doesn't want to hear that, it's your choice. You can use those memories as an excuse as to why you aren't getting on with your life in a more productive way; or see that those memories have no effect on you at all. Decide to change how you act and what you think. As you do this, the energy and vibration you send out as you co-create will be all powerful. Focusing your thoughts on positive outcomes will allow change to take place in your life no matter what your past experiences have been. Begin work today on healing all of your relationships, whether they are in your present or past. If you take responsibility for choosing your parents and children in this life, how can you carry resentments and grudges? You may not like the experiences you had, but you were the co-creator. You chose to interact for a reason. As you decide to forgive, or better still embrace all you have orchestrated and experienced, you balance karma and set yourself free from having to repeat certain themes.

I clearly remember a time when a client of mine was in a very distressing situation with her husband. This couple had been married for about seven years. And for most of those years they had a very romantic and strong connection between them. From their very first meeting, they felt as if they had known each other before. There was no doubt in their minds: they were soulmates. Their marriage was blissfully happy until their daughter was born. Her birth seemed to trigger a sense of jealousy in Claire's husband that neither of them was able to get to understand. Constant disagreements began creating distance between them, resulting in them living apart. They separated and began fighting over custody of their daughter. Claire's husband tried to gain sole custody of their daughter, claiming his wife to be an unfit mother. The husband was a psychiatrist of some reputation and was highly respected professionally. Claire tried very hard not to be revengeful and to understand why this was happening. The more she asserted herself, the more he spread rumors about her being an alcoholic. He gave support money only intermittently and generally defamed her character to anyone that would listen.

As I looked into their past lives, I saw very clearly that they had been sisters in a previous life. Claire had been the prettier sister leading to an enormous amount of jealousy between them. She was also extremely callous. Both fell in love with the same man when they were very young. When they were old enough to marry, Claire lied to him about her sister. He chose to marry Claire, and she callously flaunted her "victory."

Claire's sister was so broken hearted that she pined away, became ill and died young.

After Claire died and her soul detached from her physical body, she reviewed that lifetime. She realized how cruel she had been and decided to balance the karma. Claire came back into her sister's life, who in this lifetime, was her husband. Not being as conscious as Claire he got revenge, and she created no new negative karma with him by not reacting on his level. It was very challenging for her. By understanding the true reasons behind their strange, violent relationship, Claire was better able to rise above many of the reactive emotions to which she had previously fallen victim. As she learned about magnetic attraction, she realized how her thoughts carried a resonance that would affect him. So she continuously worked with him on an energy level. She sent messages and loving thoughts to his soul from her soul, asking that these thoughts be communicated from his soul to his conscious mind. As she gave him nothing to fuel his anger, he eventually became involved with another woman. In winning custody of his daughter, he began to have less free time to date his new love. Finally, the issue became a non-issue. Claire had won the battle, that of not re-enacting their old karmic patterns. Her ex-husband decided that he no longer wanted sole custody of their daughter, and daughter and mother were reunited.

Claire had set herself free of the negative karma between them. As a result, it would not be necessary to return in another lifetime to continue their saga. In setting herself free of a karmic debt that she had placed upon herself in self-judgment, she forgave herself and her soulmate. By releasing all judgment about it, she automatically released herself from her karmic debt.

Many times, one person is more consciously aware than the other of the agreements and commitments made throughout lifetimes. Usually, the more conscious person will take responsibility for co-creating by enabling a loving relationship. In Claire's case, she chose to work on her own karma by rising above the emotions that were causing emotional entrapment with her soulmate. Allowing a space for him to work on his own karma released her in the process.

*In this lifetime, whomever you have
a karmic connection with will once
more come into your life.*

In an abusive situation, you will almost definitely be balancing karma from a past life with that person. However, it is your vibration right now in this life that has attracted a relationship of struggle in the first place. See the correlation, and take responsibility for it. By claiming your power, you are then free to change your vibration. Change the way you feel about yourself and you change the relationship.

Take responsibility for the role you play in your relationships: in part, by understanding the law of cause/effect/cause. As a result you will find a tremendous surge of power. With this new strength and understanding, you will find the courage and determination to move away from abusive relationships. If you are in an unhealthy relationship it didn't just happen to you in a vacuum, after all. Plenty of people will be happy to tell you that you are a victim. Listen to them, and you will absolutely reinforce your feelings of being powerless. Instead, be more understanding and accepting of yourself and know you are capable of sending out a different vibration, one that does not invite abuse.

You are always free to release yourself from past relationship patterns and balance your karma in a more positive way. Don't think of it as a failure if your relationship ends in separation or divorce. Imagine two soul's in a Divine Cosmic dance. You come together for certain moves and exchanges and you drift apart. You are constantly growing and changing. So, moving on to create space for new love and joy is a positive step, not one of failure. Whatever choices you choose, let them be without judgment. Only *you* can decide what is best for you, as you listen to your Inner Wisdom.

Your Inner Wisdom never judges

Imagine that you are ready to have a broader perspective of your life. Trust for a moment that whatever you're experiencing is a result of the energy you are sending out about yourself and life. Pause for a moment and think what you most dislike about yourself. Now, change the thoughts from judgment and self-hate to acceptance and love. Feel the difference. If you can't feel it use your imagination and pretend how it would be to feel acceptance and love of self.

By making these changes, you will be sending out a completely different vibration, one that will not align itself with the energy of an abusive person. Your abusive partner will not even know what happened. He or she will suddenly and simply no longer wish to be around you. Vibrationally out of alignment with each other, your pattern will have changed. Essentially moving from elementary school to college, you will then become ready to attract and connect with a new classmate worthy of your love. Most of your lifetimes shared with your soulmates have been left as unfinished business. Why not use this lifetime to balance or transcend karma you have not yet resolved, either together or independently.

When you are balancing karma, the relationship needs to exist only as long as it takes to resolve all that you left unfinished.

When one person feels it's time to free themselves, their soul will send guidance assuring them that past karma has been balanced, and that its now okay to move on. This communication is often received on an unconscious level, so one partner may end the relationship quite abruptly, leaving the other partner in a state of shock and non- understanding. Neither party may realize that more than a present day relationship is involved. But the truth remains: the past life is interacting with the present. And the cosmic dance of life continues.

When the opportunity arises for souls to connect once again, you send out a vibration that resonates with that person with whom you are ready to further your growth. You have the choice to either remain in that relationship or to leave it. Just be sure if you choose to separate, that you've put the relationship and all of your debris connected with it into the light. As you broaden your understanding of life's purpose, you will continuously re-evaluate past decisions and beliefs. With a higher level of awareness about past lifetimes, perhaps you will not carry the same negative emotions you once had. You'll be able to understand for example, that the reasons behind your spouse's abusiveness or untrustworthiness is a matter of balancing karma, one that becomes a mirror for your own self-reflection.

Disappointment, even divorce or separation,
ultimately helps you further along
your path towards joy and love.

If you or your partner do not grow at the same pace either emotionally or spiritually, you may be together for only for a limited period of time. In the case of separation or divorce, (whether you leave your partner or he/she leaves you), understand that the relationship is not a "failure." It is simply another step along your path. And it may have been a necessary step, even a planned step set up as a probability before this lifetime. Believe it or not, it went according to plan. As you put emotional baggage *without blame* into a positive framework, you are now able to grow independently and are now ready for your next encounter. Eventually, you may be able to bless this experience as you realize the benefits you received.

Understand that this lifetime is just one of hundreds that you have lived. It gives you a slightly different perspective than believing that this life is all there is, doesn't it? Life is always full of ups and downs. Sometimes, it may become completely overwhelming. Yet; it helps to have an overview to remember the bigger picture. If you find yourself sometimes feeling lonely, sad and depressed, remember that at the right time, you <u>will</u> meet your next soulmate. Whatever you have experienced in the meantime, even if it's not what you want, is exactly what you needed. In your Divine Plan, you experience what you need for your spiritual journey.

MAGNETIC ATTRACTION

Soulmate: it means something different to everyone. And yet that longing within your heart to find and be with a soulmate is universal. Seemingly, so many others are happy and in love with their partner. But you feel left out, even jealous, fearful and insecure because you haven't yet found that special someone. And acknowledging those feelings of jealousy or hurt often bring up emotions of guilt as you chastise yourself for such immature feelings. Be aware of the uncomfortable feeling inside when you're are in the frame of mind that might lead to thoughts such as." You don't deserve to have him/her, I am nicer, (prettier, more handsome, or brighter)." The law of magnetic attraction is bound to bring more of the same uncomfortable feelings back to you. The more you indulge yourself with these types of thoughts (amplified even more by emotion), the quicker the universe will create additional situations to accentuate your feelings of jealousy.

You co-create by manifesting the power of your thoughts combined with the law of magnetic resonance. This process is constant: whether your aware of it or not. You are constantly co-creating your future at any given moment. You may dedicate yourself to consciously focusing and visualizing. However, be aware that negative thoughts manifest themselves in a negative outcome. Thinking about all that you do *not* have actually results in pushing away the happiness and loving emotions that you are craving. So you can see how important it is to watch your thoughts and make sure you are sending out positive energy towards what you *do* want instead of focusing on what you don't want.

Let the universe take care of the details.

If you practice the techniques and exercises at the end of this chapter as they'll help you change the way you look at your life. One technique to turn around a situation where you are feeling insecure is to find things to appreciate in the other people involved. Then find that appreciative feeling for yourself. Bask in that energy of all you appreciate in the other person, even if you are still feeling insecure or jealous. Send yourself feelings of appreciation for all you are, then hand your emotions and feelings to Source, and ask for its highest resolution. That flow of positive energy will create a strengthening of self-esteem.

To attract your soulmate into your life take these three steps:

• **Focus**

Focus your energy positively. Notice how many times you experience feelings of longing and emptiness when you think about the love that you do not yet have. Become aware that you are negatively focusing your energy on what is missing. Remember,that kind of focus will attract even more longing and emptiness, repelling that very person you are looking for. Thoughts of what you don't want...not wanting to feel lonely, not wanting to feel unloved or unappreciated, for example... set the forces of creation in motion. Feeling fearful that you will never find or deserve the love you long for will not attract the positive result you want. In addition, take note of how you have attracted certain types of relationships to you based on fear, worry or past beliefs. Realize the part you have played in the process.

Are you ready for change? First, focus your energy on what you do want, such as wonderful relationship with someone of your dreams. Imagine your perfect partner as a living, breathing human being only a thought away. He or she already exists. Magnetize your perfect partner to you by releasing a harmonious vibration, one that will align your partner's energy with yours.

- **Believe**

Believe that this magical union can and will happen. Vibrate an energy that will attract the next perfect partner. As you visualize and affirm that your energy fields are connecting, you will feel alive and uplifted. If you have uncomfortable feelings as you affirm, then you still have hidden beliefs that need to be cleared. Once you flow the energy of "I'm ready to love and be loved," with enthusiasm, you literally set the universe in motion. And it starts to create the circumstances necessary for your desires to happen.

- **Allow**

The third step is to allow this connection between you and your future partner to take place. The good news is that you don't have to look for your soulmate. Harmoniously send out this energy and believe the connection will happen. The universe will take care of the details.

Sometimes, because of a karmic debt, you may attract a life long love into your experience who worships the ground you walk on regardless of whether or not you feel deserving. This circumstance doesn't happen often, but sometimes is destined to be. Most of us would love to attract this type of unconditional love, but just in case that is not in your future, start working on yourself now. You need to be supportive and loving of self first so that you may cherish within the qualities that you are looking for in another, such as love, spirituality, honesty, humor, and strength. If you react in a negative way to the thought of loving yourself, then begin with the idea of really liking yourself. For most people, that is an easier way and it will gradually lead into love of self.

Whom you attract into your life
is determined by your own vibration,
and karmic lessons.

If you have worked on yourself as you read this book, you're probably now more aware of your thoughts as you daydream about your future partner, whether it is lover, husband or wife. You're not expecting to repeat old patterns in prior relationships, be they with previous lovers or friends. Instead, you're creating new, positive patterns for life's fulfillment. You're not afraid that life seems "too good to be true" and that it won't last.

Life is good and you do deserve happiness.

You're telling yourself that you are lovable just the way you are, even if you still feel that you're too fat, or thin, short or tall, or that you should be purple instead of green. If you are not yet in this place of acceptance, take the journey at the end of this chapter. It will give you a way to release yourself from any negative beliefs in conflict with your desires.

There's no need to worry that you are forcing the universe into manifesting your desires. If you try to "make" something happen in your time frame before you're ready to experience what you want, a mismatch of energy will result. Your intuition will tell you that it's not time yet and to be patient.

Let's say that you connect with your Inner Wisdom, align your vibration and visualize your soulmate in your life. But, perhaps you have your eyes–or libido—focused in the wrong place. If it doesn't feel like a "done deal," your Inner Guidance will let you know. Don't try to make something happen unless you want to set yourself up for some very challenging karmic situations with your future love. Your soul knows what's best for you, so pay attention. If you're feeling that you are trying too hard, and not flowing with your desires you are pushing. Instead, know resistance (the opposite of flow) is an indicator that you are not congruent with all you want to manifest.

LOVE IS YOUR SPIRITUAL PATH

Every relationship you have ever experienced, no matter how fleeting, has offered you a way to open your heart to learn how to love unconditionally. Love is infinitely available to all of us. It is the energy of Source, that which we breath and is filtered through every cell of our body. Love is uplifting and healing, totally unconditional. As such, it only knows compassion and forgiveness. At times, it may appear to your mind that you're experiencing a lack of love. However, know that you've created this perception with your attitudes and beliefs.

Fall head over heels in love, and that beautifully exciting, loving relationship provides the ultimate connection. But does it? We look at life through rose colored glasses while on the receiving end of unlimited adoration. We feel lovable, wonderful and special, alive and whole. Look at it this way.

> *The spark we find with someone else*
> *is really sparking self-love within.*

This self-love is something that we crave with every fiber of our being. However, we're not always consciously aware that we crave it, or even need it. Love of self closes the gap of separation that we feel from Source. We are part of that energy; nothing about us is not part of it. But so often we forget.

When you're in love, it seems so easy to give to another, especially at the beginning of a romance. Filled with joyful exuberance that seems to trigger within us that love of life, that wonder and ability to see as if with new eyes. No wonder we search so desperately for our magical counterpart, our soulmate!

Looking into the eyes of love from your soulmate, expect to feel love for self, and to feel loved and lovable. The acknowledgment allows you to feel that you can do more, and be more. Inspired by this feeling of being loved, you believe that you can do something "important." You sense that you do, indeed, have a purpose here on earth, even if you don't yet know what your specific contribution will be.

After falling in love, you may believe for a time that your sole purpose is to make your partner happy. Your level of spiritual awareness determines how long you continue to feel this priority of meeting your partner's needs over your own. Although you will still desire to see love reflected in your partner's eyes and to feel that warmth and love reflected within yourself, sooner or later it will no longer be enough.

Your spiritual quest cannot be accomplished by anyone other than yourself.

Recognizing that you are part of the Divine Source, open yourself to receive the flow of love. Sit in mediation, marvel at the magnificence of nature. Expand your energy fields and draw in the energy of love. Enjoy the overflow and share it with others. By doing so, you'll attract more of the same.

Drawing closer to an understanding of what you want from and for yourself in this life allows for an awakening. On your journey into wholeness, everything that is within you in need of transformation will be reflected back by your friends and lovers. Reflections, aspects of you that have perhaps been concealed, are now ready to surface. Recognize that you are given and give to yourself exactly what you need every step of the way to heal your heart. It's a romantic idea that when you fall in love, your partner will rescue you from all of your pain and struggle. Life is bound to be a bed of roses when in love, isn't it? If those roses also have some thorns, in hindsight you'll be able to reflect back from a perspective of detachment and understand the purpose it served from a higher viewpoint.

Taking more and more responsibility for the people you have attracted into your life better allows you to look back in your past for any unfinished business. Starting with your parents, everyone you have encountered has served a purpose. If you are harboring feelings of blame, release them. Until you do so, you will not be truly free.

Any feelings you harbor that don't feel good are not benefiting you

Take the time to heal all past memories as you take responsibility for choosing the situations and the people with whom you've connected. Some of these choices were made before you entered into this incarnation. Yet they were chosen for a purpose. We may balk in horror at the very idea of thinking loving thoughts about a certain aunt or neighbor who is always mean and nasty. But accept that they are in your life for a reason. God didn't punish you by creating them to be in your life. You co-created them to give yourself the opportunity to transcend the desire to react on their level. Unhappy people most need to receive your love. Understand it this way: it's almost a certainty that they do not have enough of it in their lives, particularly self-love. Open your heart and send your love, not necessarily directed to their personality, but to their soul essence. In doing so, you are setting yourself free from having to learn future karmic lessons with them, or others just like them. Nothing is a mistake. Everything takes us home to Source.

There is never a wrong time to call on your
intuition to ask for help.

If you ever feel the need for extra insight and support, seek it within. Your Inner Wisdom is always
available and only too happy to help you with earthly
challenges. Call upon your inner strength through
prayer or meditation. Or, simply open your heart to
connect with Source. The unconditional love and
acceptance of your Inner Guidance will help you to
release fear, insecurity, or jealousy. Connect with vibrations of your higher emotions (such as love and joy,)
filtered through Source, and a transformation of the
lower vibrations will take place.

Work with your Inner Wisdom

Listen to your Inner Wisdom by looking within to
connect with a deeper part of yourself. Use your breath
to quiet your busy mind. Your intuition will let you
know through your feelings when you are creating
what you want without conflict. Be aware of different
parts of your body through your imagination. Realize if
you are holding tension that needs to be released. As
you let go of your tension and relax, notice how this
affects your emotions. Become aware of a sense of

expansion in your energy, the feeling you have when you feel very safe and carefree.

- **Imagination**

In your imagination, picture the type of person that you wish to meet. In particular, focus on the emotional feelings that you want to share. Think about the pleasure of sharing your joy and love with someone you're connecting with on so many levels. Resonate with the matching of your desires, the connection of heart to heart, soul to soul frequencies. Use your imagination to create this feeling of connection. Tell the universe you're ready. State it out loud. "I am ready to open my heart to connect with my soulmate to give and receive love, and to share the joy of life together."

- **Intensity**

Feel passionately and with great intensity about what you wish to manifest. This passion will create an intense energy of subatomic particles, the building blocks for manifestation. Focus on the qualities within the person that you want to attract. Then if its important to you move on to their outer wrapping. The law of magnetic attraction is absolute. So, make sure that you focus on what you *do* want, not on what you *do not* want. Remember: Whatever you focus on the most is what you will get!

129

Visualize, affirm, and imagine sending out a magnetic resonance to connect with the energy of your desired mate. Next, surrender your dream to Source, so that it can manifest in the highest, best form for all concerned. Don't concentrate on attracting your soulmate if you feel sad, lonely or depressed, however. In those times of need your energy vibration is low and slow, and heavy. You'll be sending out conflicting messages with opposing vibrations. One energy will be what you want and the other energy will be what you don't have.

Change your energy before you consciously co-create by doing something that you enjoy. Dance, listen to music, walk on the beach, or work out. Let yourself experience whatever makes you feel strong and uplifted. When you've allowed yourself to feel good, start your visualization and affirmations. Thank the universe as if you already have what you want

Your relationships are assignments from God

As you become clearer about your thoughts and what you want from a relationship, you will become more responsible for the type of person you attract into your life. At various stages, you'll place emphasis on one aspect over another. The type of person you attract will change based on your focus, be it physical, mental, emotional or spiritual. But wherever you are along your path of experience, know that you <u>will</u> bring into your life the right person who will act as the perfect catalyst to help you peel away more layers and open your heart.

You might decide to create a relationship from a purely physical or emotional level. If you do so without focusing on a spiritual level and by refusing to listen to your Inner Wisdom you'll probably learn some difficult lessons. In that case, the mate that you attract into your life may be very exciting physically. Yet mentally and spiritually you may be mis-matched. This imbalance will create a very uneven relationship full of polarities, which in turn creates much disagreement. Your life becomes so much easier when you work hand in hand with your soul, especially when it concerns your soulmate.

Inner Wisdom loves you unconditionally.

Self-judgment and criticism can cause you to believe you are not worthy of—or ready for—a connection with your Inner Wisdom. Self-judgment can also make you feel that you are not deserving of this Divine connection. Judgment is very insidious and feels very sticky, doesn't it? Even when you think you've released it, sometimes it creeps in through the back door.

Learn how to transform your judgment into acceptance by giving yourself more space to feel and to live with joyful, unconditional love. Without judgment there is acceptance of all you are at this very moment. Accept yourself and shout to the universe "I am okay, I am perfect in my seeming imperfection." The more you focus on being okay, the more okay you will feel. And it doesn't matter if you feel you are making it up. Do it anyway; the universe doesn't know the difference.

Your intuition is an Inner Wisdom that is always with you and guiding you. Accept that as a fact. Know also, that you don't have to feel worthy in order to communicate with your Inner Wisdom. You are worthy because you exist. It is your Divine right to access this guidance. As part of your energy, your Inner Wisdom does not judge you. It simply loves you and allows you to learn at your own pace. Feel the relief in knowing that you don't have to be perfect. You are perfect, right now. And you are also right where you are meant to be in your journey through life. Your soul continually yet gently directs you into different situations that give you exactly what you need in each and every moment. Learn to trust the process. Learn to trust your intuition. It will guide you through every thought and decision, helping you to see what no longer serves you.

Soulmates resonate at a similar frequency

The next important person in your life will radiate the same magnetic qualities that are within you. As you consciously co-create a connection, sooner or later you will be led to one another to have a karmic experience. If you are truly happy with yourself, you will find great similarities with your soulmate. And if you establish a connection physically, emotionally, mentally as well as a spiritually, you've probably found your "quintessential soulmate." Most probably, you will both think and feel passionately alike, about life and spirituality. You will find great pleasure in lovemaking, and will have a deep soul to soul connection that allows for transference of thoughts and feelings, often without words.

The more you resonate compatibly with your partner, the more harmonious your lives will be. You don't stop growing and learning simply because you have found your "dream soulmate." Instead, you now have the opportunity to facilitate each other's growth, as well as your own, through love and laughter. Your lives will flow easily as you share the desire for spiritual growth, combined with the enjoyment of many of the same hobbies and commonalties of thinking. You will not spend so much of your energy trying to work through dis-similarities with your partner. Instead, you will have more time and energy to be creative and to help others, if that is what you desire to do.

The more you share with others and connect with your own intuition, the more your life moves with synchronicity and the more you will receive.

The law of cause and effect, which is really effect creates cause, never stops working. If you want love, you need to give love. The more you give, the more you will attract back. Think about it: If you sit around and feel sorry for yourself because no one loves you, yet all you think about is yourself, why would anyone even want to love you. A selfish, self-absorbed energy is not very attractive to others. And it's not likely that anyone will want to rescue you from feeling that way.

Josie had been searching for love for a long time and hadn't had a date in years. At our session, she complained that no one seemed attracted to her. According to her, men were only interested in pretty women, with "Playboy bodies." As we talked, it was apparent (even to Josie) that she hated herself and the way she looked.

She even seemed to go out of her way to make herself unattractive to others. Alas, this was a reflection of how she felt within.

I explained how our magnetic thoughts attract back to us more of the same. Yet Josie did not want to take responsibility for the type of people she was meeting. She was stuck in a rut, pointing her finger and blaming others. Josie expected me to make everything right with her love life. Unfortunately, I was unable to help her. Until and unless she can take responsibility for all she is attracting, her love life will not change for the better. Sometimes, people have to hit rock bottom before they decide out of desperation that change is needed.

When Josie changes her viewpoint to see her pleasant qualities and begins to like herself, she has a chance of attracting someone who cares for her. Right now, her focus is on disliking herself and disliking the way "all men are." As a result, her energy is giving her exactly what she is focused on—more of the same.

The more loving and joyful we are with others and ourselves, the more desirable we will be. And, the more we will attract someone to us to share our love. The exchange of energy is an immutable law. By participating, we open our hearts to feel and express our essence. In doing so, we remember ourselves as spiritual beings connected to Source.

***The road to self-love and the healing of your heart,
so desirable a journey is often a path full of obstacles***

You have now reached an understanding of the "perfection" of your life and how your path will always take you ultimately, to the joy and happiness that you desire. As a co-creator of your experience it is entirely up to you what type of person you attract into your life, and what type of path you create on the journey. Some paths are rockier than others with many obstacles along the way. Some are more routine, even boring. Some are exhilarating, and others are scenic and beautiful. The more conscious you become, the more you will attract a person of similar consciousness, where your journey becomes easier and more peaceful. Feel excited by the possibilities. You are powerful; your future is in your hands. Somewhere, your soulmate is waiting for you. Everyone who desires it has a soulmate–including you!

JOURNEY TO CONNECT WITH
YOUR SOULMATE

Turn within and allow yourself to take a few deep breaths. Now, place your awareness in your heart area. Imagine the emotional condition of your heart. Do you feel or sense that it is damaged, or cold, or padlocked? With your inner eyes and senses, imagine you are cradling your heart in your hands. Around your hands are two hands of Light. Let this healing power of Source pour into your hands and into your heart. Imagine your heart becoming healed and place it back inside your body.

Visualize a large, open silver box to the side of you. Let all of your negativity connected with relationships—feelings of not deserving, betrayal, or abandonment—come out of you into the box. When you are ready and have released enough, close down the lid of the box and push it behind you into your past. As it moves out of view, your focus is now off these thoughts.

Now, think thoughts that make you feel happy, powerful, joyful and alive. Focus on letting that emotion flood through your body. Think as intensely as you can of the love that you wish to bring into your life. Imagine giving and receiving this love equally. Feel it in your heart so intensely it is as if your heart is singing. It's so passionately ready. Now imagine a magnetic coil in your heart that is beginning to spin. As it spins, it begins to expand, and it widens as it rotates, ever expanding until it is rotating around the outside of your body, sending out a magnetic resonance. Continue to let it rotate in ever widening circles farther and farther out, way beyond where you can see. You are sending out a frequency that will attract the same frequency. Let this energy continue to expand until it connects with the energy of your soulmate. Hold the intensity for at least thirty-three seconds, or until you feel a definite connection. When you get this connection, it is time to reverse the spin of the magnetic coil. It now has the energy of your quintessential soulmate as it spins towards you. Slowly becoming smaller and smaller as it comes closer and closer into your energy fields, pulling it right into your heart. Give thanks to Source and then let it go. By letting it go and not continuing to "make it happen" you are handing it over to a higher power to come to you in the best possible way for all concerned.

Do this exercise as many times as you want. But it's best if you don't put a specific person into your co-creation. When co-creating, it's very important to not interfere in anyone else's karma. If you find it impossible not to focus on a particular person, then bless the interaction by adding. "Let it happen so that it for the highest benefit of all concerned." That way, you are letting the universe have the final say. After all, from our limited perspective, how can we possible see what's in our best interests? Our Inner Wisdom always has an overview of the bigger picture of our life's purpose, and always knows what's best for us.

Chapter Four

CHOOSING FINANCIAL ABUNDANCE

Most of us dream of being financially abundant, of having material prosperity. Our dreams are to have enough money to never worry about paying our bills. We imagine how it will feel to be able to buy anything our hearts desire. We think about taking trips around the world, or how it will feel to donate huge amounts of money to charities or give to individuals to help them have a better life. We all want the feeling and security of knowing that we don't have to worry about paying the rent, or wondering how to put our children through college. We want not only the material securities but the non-material benefits that come from having an abundant supply of money, feelings of peace of mind, a sense of security, and happiness.

It is not selfish to have desires, of wanting more. There is a fine division between being dissatisfied with what you have and feeling ungrateful, which comes more from a place of fear: or desiring more from a place of gratitude.

Become aware of how you have tried to create more abundance.

You have asked the universe for it, prayed for it, used visualizing techniques, and still it has not flowed into your life. If this is your situation you are probably trying to manifest it like most people, from a place of lack, fear, or anxiety about not having it. When you want more than you have, and you feel you have got to have it, it places your vibration in a lower vibration of fear and need. It creates great stress within and creates a disconnection from your Inner Wisdom and the abundance flow. In fact, craving wealth from a place of lack will lessen your ability to manifest abundance, as you will not be in vibrational harmony with your desire. The universe responds to your desire of wanting financial abundance, and also responds to your focus on not having enough financial abundance. Remember that as you send out the message "I want" the universe supports you in wanting and you get more wanting. As you focus on not having you get more of it. No wonder you are struggling!

Counting your blessings and placing yourself in alignment with happiness and gratitude will aid you in magnetizing prosperity.

So how do you change your energy, and become grateful? As you take responsibility for being the creator of your life and co-creator with Source, you begin to see that you can have abundance in any area you want. You can open yourself up to receive miracles. It is your Divine right as part of the Source to create for yourself anything you want that will uplift you and help you to uplift others. All you need to know is how to clear the debris that creates resistance in you so that you allow your connection with the abundance stream.

Who do you believe is your source of abundance? You might ask yourself if you believe that you are the source of your abundance, or do you believe that your spouse or job or parent is your source? If you believe that the source of financial freedom lies outside of yourself, you are not tapping into the wealth that becomes available to you if you connect to your Inner Wisdom.

Wealth first comes from within.

You will feel reassured once you master this process of connecting with the unlimited abundance stream and believe that you can always access it. Then, no matter what happens in the world economy, you will be able to attract wealth.

Learning how to manifest and become proficient at aligning your energy allows you to be filled with a sense of aliveness. As you indulge yourself thinking about the way you want to live, and know that you play a part in allowing it to come to you, you experience feelings that are quite joyful. Co-creating is part of a process of allowing yourself to feel unlimited as you connect with ever expanding visions of accomplishment.

When you say you want more money, what you are really looking for is the feeling of security and freedom and peace of mind that having more than enough money would allow you to experience. Most people know that having money and the ability to buy anything you want will not automatically fill the void that may be inside you. It does not mean that all of your needs will be met, or that you will love yourself. It will not provide you with inner peace if you are not happy with who you are, although it will take pressure off you to know that you can pay your bills on time.

HIDDEN AGENDAS

There are any number of different reasons why you may not let yourself connect with the abundance stream. If you want to release yourself from these blocks it is necessary to find out what hidden and sometimes not so hidden beliefs you have about money. Lets take a look at some of the ones that I come across most often. One of the most prevalent is not really believing that you deserve it, you may hold on to the idea that you have not worked hard enough, or you are not bright enough, or someone else deserves it more than you do.

I notice when I play the lottery I always find myself thinking, "I cannot win too much money because there are so many more people who need it more than I do." With this belief that I don't seem to want to change, there is no way I am going to win a huge amount playing the lottery. I am fully aware of my conflicting thoughts. If and when I am ready, I will change them. I also understand intellectually that there is an abundance of abundance! My having is not taking away from anyone—yet somewhere inside of me I have not yet changed my old beliefs about "not enough to go around."

This may be one of the reasons you may not allow yourself financial success. Perhaps you are concerned that if you have plenty of money, someone else will go without. You may feel that you are being greedy if you want more. That is as silly as thinking that if you breath too much oxygen, you are taking some away from other people. You never think about that source of energy not being abundant, so why do you think about money in a limited way? It is all a form of energy, available to all of us all the time, if we use enthusiasm to energize the universal law of abundance.

I do often see that people carry poverty consciousness with them from past lives, and it does affect them in this life until they decide to change their thinking about money. It is your thoughts right now on the subject that are setting up your future.

Ginny was a very wealthy heiress who had inherited her millions from a father who had grown up in the depression. During those years he had lost all his money, and then came back to make more than ever. He had always instilled in Ginny the idea that you can lose your money at the drop of a hat. He had seen a few of his associates commit suicide during the depression years because of financial ruin, and had convinced himself that happiness depended on a huge bank account. Ginny had adopted his fear of losing money and actually felt she could never have enough–in case something went "wrong." Ginny had a poverty consciousness. Yet her karma in this lifetime was not connected with finances, but her challenge she had set herself was to be able to let money flow in and out without attachment. Ginny was also unhappy in her relationships, and as you might guess was not very open and loving to others. She had this feeling that everything she wanted had to be held on to with an attitude of mine, mine, mine. And she had come to the realization that money was not going to buy her happiness, although she really wanted to change she did not know how.

As she gradually absorbed the idea that her thoughts were creating her unhappy life, and that money could not buy what she was looking for she began to relax a little. As Ginny released her fear of losing everything that she had believed would give her happiness, she began to see a bigger picture. One that showed her that caring for others and opening her heart to find love and joy were far more likely to bring her what she wanted to experience than being closed and selfish would. She began to view money as a form of energy, and began seeing her thoughts and feelings as energy as well. Ginny started to give her money to various causes and people in need, and found the rewards coming back to her from the hearts of others.

If someone else had Ginny's fear of losing money as well as having karmic lessons connected with prosperity, they would probably have lost the money altogether. In Ginny's case, the karmic lesson she had set up for herself around money, was to lead her to a deeper lesson about love and trust. In her next phase of learning and understanding, Ginny will probably be able to trust that someone can love her for herself and not for her money, providing another giant leap towards her wholeness.

Like so many people Ginny did not realize that it was not money itself that she wanted, it was what money represented and could buy that she desired. She wanted security, and stability, and the need to feel safe. She believed that without money it was impossible to have those feelings. And, as she became aware that feeling safe came from a deeper inner connection with Source, she realized a new way to feel both secure and centered. Trusting this new wisdom allowed her to adopt a new perspective on life.

Before you start to send out your energy to magnetize abundance you need to be very clear about what you really do want to attract into your life.

- What is the essence of what you want from having an abundant amount of money?

    What qualities are you looking for in your life?
- What needs will it fulfill?

If you decide that you want a high paying job so that you can start to invest your extra money in the stock market or real estate, it helps to have an idea of what you want in and around this new job. If your focus is only on a high salary as you visualize, you may find a job that pays you an enormous salary, but find yourself working with people who are not in harmony with you. You may find that you are driving to far to work in rush hour, or that the position brings too much stress with it. If you are clear about your requirements as you think about your new high paying job, you will include your happiness and well being as part of your vision. Ultimately your new job is your way to spiritual growth, therefore, creating a situation that is harmonious in all areas will allow you to expand and learn through pleasure rather than struggle.

Some of you may want to create a way to make money that still allows you plenty of time off to enjoy your hobbies. You may not know exactly what type of job would allow you to do that. As you think about that style of life, let the universe feel your desire for happiness, joy, creativity and abundance. If you want to work helping others in some capacity, include that in your vision as you send out your desires to the universe. Don't tie yourself up in knots because you don't know exactly what you want to do. It is the feeling behind your desire that the universe responds to, so let the universe take care of the details. Just make sure you are feeling good about your request.

If you find yourself wanting a new high paying job remember to imagine that it already exists. Pretend you already have it as you send that energy to Source. Become aware if you are also thinking any negative thoughts, such as. "Who would want to pay me so much money." You know what will happen if you have "yes, but's."

As you get the mindset that the abundance stream is always there for you to tap into, it will take enormous pressure off you. So often you may find yourself working from the opposite position, where you may be thinking "I don't have enough money to pay my medical bill, or my rent/mortgage, or my alimony, so I need to manifest money right now." If you try to create anything positive into your life as you come from a place of not having enough, which is really just a place of fear and anxiety, you will be totally out of vibrational harmony with your desires. You will only manifest more of what you don't want, as that is the vibration most prevalent within you caused by the focus of "I don't have." The poorer you feel, the poorer you become. This becomes a great catch twenty-two. When you need something to change the most in your life or pocket book, it is the very time you cannot co-create it, so what do you do?

Choose to think thoughts that create a
feeling of aliveness and joy.

You need to find something to do that shifts your energy. Something which allows you to feel uplifted and strong. Music can often transport you into this state of enjoyment, or perhaps dancing, or working out at the gym. Running or walking outside in nature are other useful methods for raising your spirits. Basically, anything that works for you which allows you to feel expanded and alive will do. Then, when you are feeling happier and stronger it is the perfect time to start sending out the magnetic energy of your desires to Source. You will be setting up the link, and letting the universe know exactly what it is you wish to co-create and attract to you. As you do this manifesting process it should be easy and feel good. If it seems that you are making it up or it is uncomfortable then you need to work with your beliefs and hidden agendas. Those uncomfortable feelings are letting you know that something is not in agreement with your vision, and that you are not in vibrational harmony with your Inner Wisdom and your desires.

I practice co-creating on a regular basis, and while writing this book I manifested something I really wanted for my thirty-first wedding anniversary. It was a diamond bracelet to symbolize all of the brilliant years my husband and I had spent together—but it was out of our price range. As I looked at it in the window of the jewelry store, I clearly told the universe that I really wanted it, and at the same time I felt that on some level it was already mine. I returned to the same jewelers four or five times. Each time I put the bracelet on my wrist even though at that moment I could not afford it, I felt that it was definitely my bracelet.

The day before our anniversary I paid one more visit to the jewelers, and was miraculously informed that the bracelet was now half price! I remember the sense of gratitude that flooded through me, and very importantly, I also noticed that I wasn't surprised. (I am actually surprised when what I focus on does not happen.) As it turned out, on my anniversary I had the bracelet on my wrist for good–what perfect timing.

As I consciously sent my desire into the universe, I knew that it was not my business to know how I was going to get my bracelet. It was only my business to send a powerful enough message so that the universe would bring it to me somehow. In countless ways throughout my life I have used this manifesting process again and again. Had I been concerned about not being able to afford it, or had I spent time worrying about where the money would come from, or entertained thoughts of being greedy or not deserving, I am sure it would not have been made available to me.

I also made certain that I was in the frame of mind where I was not attached to having to have it. I do this, by handing it over to Source to come in its highest form for the best of all concerned. By releasing attachment, I did not set up a negative flow that would cancel out or repel the manifestation I wanted to create in the first place.

LOOKING AT YOUR THOUGHTS

If everything you desire to have in your life already exists, then why oh why doesn't everyone have financial prosperity? Hidden agendas offer some of the reasons you may not be manifesting what you want, but there may be other reasons. Is it possible that you are simply not allowing it to come to you. Can it really be that you are the reason you are struggling financially? What could you possible be doing that would keep you from allowing abundance to be part of your life?

One of the most challenging parts of mastering the manifesting process is accepting that if you are struggling financially, you have unconsciously chosen it. You do not consciously want struggle, yet it is exactly what you need at this moment otherwise it would not be part of your life. Source does not make mistakes, so we must always remember that everything we find in our lives happens for a reason. If we think of the universe as being our source of prosperity, Source becomes our banker, our checkbook, our manager, and our Inner Wisdom becomes the link with this energy of manifestation. With this new idea, the thoughts of "there is nobody else to help me pay my bills, it's all up to me," will virtually become obsolete, and the abundance that is always around you will become a very tangible energy.

Lack is an illusion.

There are many beliefs you may hold on to that you have picked up throughout your life that affect your thoughts, and your thoughts combined with feeling determine what you co-create. In your manifestation process, the first road block you may set up for yourself is, that you do not necessarily believe that abundance is yours for the asking. You also may not believe that you can really co-create, especially if you have not had too much success so far tapping into the abundance stream. Another part of you may not feel you deserve to have a lot of money, or still you may believe you are taking away from someone else more deserving, if asking for prosperity for yourself. It is even possible on a deep level to be afraid of being wealthy, for it might bring judgment and envy from others, and you may not want to pay that price.

Will you be different if you are wealthy? How will you be different? Is it really true that you will be different, or will you still be the same person? Get in touch with your beliefs about what money means to you. Find out if you think that it will boost your self-esteem, and if so, does that tell you that you feel insecure about yourself?

These are only a few of the numerous reasons that create struggle around money issues. I know for myself one of the hidden reasons that I only allowed myself a certain level of success was an unconscious program that I had accepted from my father. I clearly remember sitting on my fathers lap and could hear him tell me. "You don't have to worry your pretty little head about money. Daddy will always take care of you, then you will get married and your husband will also take care of you." Well consciously I had certainly not held on to that old fashioned idea, yet when I was pulling all of my beliefs out into the open, there it was. It is amazing what you will discover as you work with undoing your limiting beliefs in all areas of your life.

If you don't have enough money in your life, you are literally saying on some level that you are not allowing it, and until you do you cannot create it. You are pushing it away, delaying your experience of it until a later date when you may be more accepting. Ask yourself, what beliefs would a person have to have to create struggle with money? Look at the answers that pop into your head. It will be different for each person based on your past relationship to money and beliefs accepted from family and friends.

You may find you have a belief that says "If I have a lot of money how will I ever know if people want to be with me for myself, or if they are only after me because of my money?" If this sounds familiar, ask yourself another question. Do you believe you are lovable and deserving of being loved for your own worth? You see, only if there is some doubt about how lovable you feel, would it even occur to you that someone might want you for your money. Examine this idea. If you really loved yourself, would it enter your head that someone would ever want to use you? The answer is no, because you would place such a high value upon

155

yourself, that you would assume others would as well. Take this example and sit for a moment and use the thoughts you have about others to reflect back to you areas within yourself you are not completely comfortable with.

The universe wants you to have everything you desire that is in alignment with your inner vibration.

Money is a way to spiritually awaken, and it is neither right or wrong. It is just another energy source. You may manifest prosperity through others who come into your life, who in some way bring you closer to your Inner Wisdom. They aid you in your understanding of abundance, as it comes through the vehicle of relationships. Other people can be very useful tools to help strip away your limiting beliefs to see that everything is indeed bringing you home to Source.

Doug was sitting with me in a very disgruntled mood. He had once more been offered a higher paying job and this would be the third time in five years that he was changing companies. Doug was never well liked at his places of employment, and he often focused on what was wrong with the people that worked for him and the people he worked for. He was very bright and accomplished at what he did for a living, but he was always looking for greener pastures. When he came to me, he had convinced himself one more time that a higher paying position in a different company would be the answer to his unhappiness. He absolutely did not want to take responsibility for his part in his unhappy work situation. He had a very strong desire to make a lot of money and certainly had the ability to do so, yet used his power and focus to see problems instead of solutions. As he reflected on what was wrong, he simultaneously reinforced the weakness in those around him. As he pushed against what he didn't like he received more of it. Most importantly, each time Doug moved on to a different company he had taken all his negative feelings with him, and re-created the same environment in each new location.

When he finally allowed himself not to be defensive, he began to look at what he was creating through his old patterns. Taking responsibility for his life without blaming others was a very new idea for him. I pointed out the perfection of all those working situations where he refused to see his higher self had been offering him opportunity after opportunity to change his perspective and his life. With this new viewpoint he could see what he had previously viewed as bad luck in the work field, as wonderful opportunities for growth. I emphasized that the more Doug reflected on all the positive aspects of his past jobs, the more he would begin to attract a new vibration and allow a different outcome into his energy fields. It takes a little time to turn ones thinking around to see what is uplifting instead off what is a downer, but now he knows how to recognize the uncomfortable feelings as clues that he is out of harmony with his Inner Guidance. Doug knows that his uncomfortable thoughts bring him experiences he would like to see eradicated from his life, and this instant feedback allows him to change the forward movement of this self-created negativity. And having brought his destructive habits to light, he will now be free of the baggage that he had dragged with him for so many years.

The lesson here is that changing jobs or spouses is not necessarily the solution to a problem, but rather, looking at which attitudes and beliefs are creating the apparent problems for you in the first place. The universe is exact, and you will continue to recreate the same type of uncomfortable situations to you again and again until the root of the problem, which will be found in your beliefs or attitudes, is recognized and changed through conscious thoughts and actions.

To create change quickly, first adopt an attitude of
thankfulness for all the good which has come
from the situation, and then send out
new energy for the way you want it to be.

Have you ever said "I want to be financially abundant," or "I want to be wealthy?" Most of us have. When we say "I want," it means we don't have. What happens is the universe doesn't sort out what you want or don't want. It is exact in following your wishes. Energetically it receives your wishing and wanting more money. It wants to give you everything you want. You are wanting more and it gives you more wanting! You want more abundance–it will give you more wanting abundance.

What you need to do, is appreciate that you already have what you desire. Yes, at this point you are making it up, acting as if. What you are thinking about may not have gathered enough density to manifest physically in your life, but you need to know you have it. You could send words similar to these into the universe. "Thank you for the experiences that are presently in my life, for I know they are here for my higher good. I appreciate all that I have and now send out an energy to connect with a greater vision of all I desire." Here you would speak about the financial abundance you are grateful for, or the perfect job, or abundant clients.

Remember to imagine how wonderful you will feel as you think about large amounts of cash being in your life. Be open to whatever way the universe wants to supply it. Say it as if it is a <u>done deal</u>.

UNLIMITED FLOWS EXIST

Soon you will come to know that Source <u>is</u> your source of abundance. You will remember that this same energy also makes up who you are, as well as being the energy of bank notes. Thinking this way helps you to think of money as being unlimited. The abundance stream is pure energy, and is always available to everyone. It does not discriminate and decide if you have earned your way to affluence by being "good." It is impartial and non-judgmental, it only responds to your intense thoughts and emotions by reflecting back to you the many opportunities and events that make up your life.

Inner prosperity attracts outer prosperity.

As you choose your family and the circumstances you wish to encounter in this life, it's up to you to take your own power and learn how to work with energy. Whether you chose to be born into a poor or wealthy family you have the same ability to connect to the abundance stream. It is available to and for everyone. It does not matter if you have only a dollar in your pocket or a million dollars. The amount of money you have at present does not change your ability to connect with this flow. It is your feeling of being abundant that allows the connection to be made. When you realize that you are abundant, not because you have a few million dollars in the bank but because you are connected with Source energy, your prosperity within enhances prosperity externally.

The universe will re-arrange itself around your ideas of how wealthy you are, when you establish within the feeling that you already have what you are asking for. Sometimes this is hard to do, yet think of it this way and perhaps it will become easier. What you are asking for already exists, and so, if you are asking for it without feeling that it is your Divine right to have it, you are disconnecting from the flow that is always available. This is a form of self-denial that will certainly keep you from tapping that source. Don't allow yourself for one moment to entertain the thought that there is something wrong with wanting to be prosperous, unless you enjoy feeling stressed about there never being quite enough in your life. Tap into that universal stream of prosperity instead, as you acknowledge that you are a Divine child of a loving Creator and the universe only wants you to be happy and fulfilled.

JOURNEY TO CONNECT WITH ABUNDANCE

Close your eyes, and imagine a large old fashioned kitchen scale in front of you. Choose a basket either on the right or left side to place all of your negative feelings and thoughts connected with prosperity.

- Put in your fears of not making enough money, or of losing your job.
- Thoughts of money being un-spiritual.
- Beliefs that there is a scarcity of money, or that it is selfish or greedy to want a lot of money.
- Put in your doubts that you are able to co-create more money. Worries that you will never make ends meet.
- Whatever you can think of that passes through your mind that is limiting you in any way.

Notice in your minds eye how the scale is now heavy on the side of your negative thoughts. Don't judge what you see. This is a journey to increase your awareness so that you can change your habit of negative thinking. Now in the other basket place your strong desire to have more money.

- Add how wonderful you will feel when you have tapped into the abundance flow.

- Ask yourself how strongly you believe you deserve to receive prosperity. If you feel you do not deserve it then it goes into the negative side, if you feel positive about it place it in the positive side.

- Put every good feeling and thought you have into the positive basket and notice without any judgment which side has the most power.

The heavier basket will let you know how you have been thinking and you will see what type of future you have been creating.

On the same side as the negative basket almost out of view behind you there is a large silver box, let yourself see or feel it in your imagination. Go over to the negative side of the scale and start taking out you fears and limiting beliefs and place them in the silver box. Take out all your thoughts that were setting you back until the basket is empty. Close down the lid of the silver box and push it behind you out of view, so that your focus is taken off all that was in the box. Now look at the scale and notice how the positive side with all the uplifting thoughts has gained in strength.

- Think of what makes you feel lighthearted, strong and happy.
- Imagine yourself dancing or listening to music.
- Walking on the beach or riding a horse or motor bike.
- Working out at the gym, or running.
- Whatever makes you feel good.

Let yourself be filled with these uplifting feelings, and in your own words, affirm to the Universe. "In this now moment, I am receiving unlimited abundance flowing into my life. I imagine enormous amounts of money in my savings account, so that I may spend it or give it away anywhere that I choose. I now harmonize my energy with the abundance stream and open to receive. Thank You Universe."

Chapter Five

THE JOY OF LIFE

Joy is a natural state of being. It sometimes seems such a fleeting state of existence and yet when you are joyful you feel so wonderful that you are completely full when experiencing it. Joy is not an emotion like happiness, which is determined by the experiences you are having and how you are reacting to them, but rather it is a state of being that you connect with on a very deep level. Joy is like being filled with an over-whelming feeling of love as if a million little bubbles are floating through your body. It is a vibration that surrounds everyone at all times and is always available for you to connect with. Joy creates a wonderful feeling of expansion within as you feel yourself connected to Source, as it is part of your creative core.

Do you have joy in your life now? Do you know what makes you feel joyful? Or, is it something nebulous somewhere out there that you will experience when you have time, or when your life changes? It seems so easy to fall into patterns of thoughts and emotions that if focused on long enough simply become a part of your daily routine. Perhaps you feel overwhelmed with all your responsibilities and find yourself living with negative feelings of, fear, anger, anxiety, blame, or worry. When this way of life becomes habitual it becomes difficult to think that it is possible to change the way you feel so that you can become happier and more joyful. Most people want to, yet do not know how, so you just get used to feeling the way you do.

Somewhere along the way you may convince yourself that if you worry about something you are keeping yourself from the trouble that would be there if you didn't worry. You may wake up each morning expecting to feel heavy or down, or feel that you are struggling to keep your head above water. When you get used to living with these feelings, you are quite aware that your heart is heavy and you are certainly aware that you don't feel joyful. Often, you don't always know what is going on inside that is keeping you from feeling more positive and becoming happier. No matter what your situation, it is your thoughts about your situation that cause your pain. As you become clearer in your understanding of the law of magnetic attraction the more obvious it becomes that you need to reframe your thoughts to begin to change the events in your life.

When Penny came to see me she was exuding a

mixed bag of emotions. The last time I saw her she was happily married, had a good job and was convinced that she did not want to have any children. As I gave her a reading, I mentioned that the spirit energy of two children were here in the room with her. I always let my clients know that these children are a probable future, not an absolute, for we can always exercise our free will. Before we incarnate into this physical form, we make certain decisions with other souls to come together once again to further our growth and perhaps balance our karma with them. This is always true of family members, yet we can change circumstances around once we are down here.

At our last meeting Penny was sure she did not want to have any children. Now, two years later, she was absolutely sure that she wanted to have a child. She had been trying to get pregnant for the last six months. As we talked about how ready she was to start a family she was bubbling with excitement. She was sure a baby would bring more joy into their lives, and her husband was equally excited. There did not seem to be any ambivalence at all about starting a family. She had made a decision and was ready!

Penny talked about trying to get pregnant, and how each month she tried to stay positive, yet felt a sadness when she found out yet again it had not happened. Unknowingly, Penny was sending out mixed messages into the universe. Her joy at the thought of having a baby was in complete alignment with her Inner Being, and through her emotions she was probably already setting the process in motion. Yet her fear of not getting pregnant, and her need and attachment to being pregnant, were sending out signals to the universe of "not pregnant, not pregnant." The law of magnetic attraction, was bringing her more of the same. The two opposing energies were canceling each other out, and prolonging the situation for her.

As time went by Penny focused more and more on not being pregnant, and she started noticing all the other pregnant women in the market and on the streets. She had previously worked on accepting that her thoughts create reality, yet she had slipped in her monitoring of them over the last few years. She realized as we talked that she was not relaxed and trusting enough about this situation, so she decided to change her focus.

Everyday at least once a day, we set up the exercise for Penny to send these words with powerful emotion out into the universe: "Universe, in this now moment I imagine the joy I feel as I carry a new life in my womb. I see the pleasure on my husbands face as I tell him the wonderful news, and I am filled with excitement as I allow this feeling of being pregnant to flood through my body. I know that the soul of my future child already exists and all I have to do is expand in trust and knowingness that we are ready to come together on a soul to soul level. I surrender this vision to you God to come in its highest form possible that is best for all concerned."

As Penny affirmed and imagined being pregnant she did it with such conviction and a sense of knowingness, that she really had not a shred of doubt that it would happen. It was equally important that after affirming, she let go of thinking about it, and go about her life as happily as she could.

It has always been known that people who seemingly could not conceive, after adopting a baby often found themselves pregnant. This is a perfect example of how trying too hard with attachment to the outcome, creates an opposing energy. Once the negative focus is off not conceiving, and the attachment and need has been released, the universe gives you what you desire.

Penny called a few weeks after that last session to say that she had just come back from the doctors office and she had tested positive for pregnancy. She was on cloud nine. By changing her thoughts and her focus from thinking about not yet being pregnant, to one of imagining herself being pregnant, she had indeed created exactly what she wanted.

Penny is now working on the thought that she and her husband may want to create a second added joy into their lives. My guidance has already shown me that is a very high probable future, and it will not be too far behind the first "joy," before he enters this world.

Sometimes a karmic agreement imposed by self before entering this lifetime will be programmed into your unconscious, and it may be that you have chosen not to give yourself children in this lifetime. If that is part of the learning and growth that you have set up for yourself, then you may have to honor the perfection of that choice. Even if it is painful, you accept and understand that the universe does not make mistakes.

So the process to observe again, is that when Penny felt down, she was in a state of contraction and density. The emotions of fear, doubt, and anxiety she was experiencing when she focused on not being pregnant, were signals to her that her thinking was not congruent with her desires. She was receiving the signal that she was creating more of what she didn't want.

Alignment leads to joy.

When you first make a decision to do your affirmations to change the way you think and feel, you are starting off with a low slow vibration which is the vibration of the reality that you are at present experiencing–not having. As you intensely imagine your vision of wanting to feel joyful and light, your desire is to connect with an energy that is high and wonderful. As you do this visualization and affirmation, you may not have raised your own physical vibration to match the one that you want to align with. This mis-match of energy is one of the reasons why your prayers and dreams are not always answered.

If you say the words and think the thoughts, yet nothing seems to change, and you still don't feel wonderful, remember, that it is the *feeling* behind the thoughts that allows the universe to respond to your requests. If you are saying something yet your feelings do not match what you are asking for, then you are not going to connect with what you want.

To raise your physical vibration first think about
something in your life either past or present
where you felt happy and joyful.

Really let yourself feel those emotions. It's necessary to imagine it with as much emotion as you can create, and pretend until you can get the bubbly high feeling that begins to connect you with the vibration of joy. It is an inner feeling, and as you connect with that flow that is always available to you, you move into a state of expansion. You are really tapping into the experience of feeling one with all life. That feeling is made up of love and joy. Everyone is made up of the same "stuff" and everyone therefore is part of the energy of Source, and has the frequency of joy available to them.

Where you stand in your life and in your consciousness right now has been determined by your ability to either expand in love, awareness and joy, or contract into fear, distrust, and blame. You are constantly being offered the chance to open your heart and connect, or you can be so busy and overwhelmed that you do the opposite. If you find yourself trapped by your circumstances, whether connected with love, finances or health, ask why did you get yourself into this pickle?

*Remember you do not have to deserve joy, it is
your Divine right to participate in that energy.*

No matter what circumstances you chose to experience in this lifetime, you are offering yourself a way to rise above the way of life that has you unconsciously co-creating more pain and suffering. You now have the knowledge of how to transform it into one of taking your power, co-creating consciously–and turning your life around.

You can now release old beliefs that keep you imprisoned emotionally, and decide that every experience coming your way is neither good or bad but a delightful opportunity to evolve and awaken. As this becomes a natural way of thinking, you begin to strengthen your connection with your Inner Wisdom. A loving attitude towards yourself and others in life will connect you with that flow of wonderful feelings that allows you to experience joy.

How would it feel to you if you could love yourself no matter what you were doing? Is that a possible goal for you? If you do want to open your heart to love and joy, yet you find yourself expressing anger, notice it, and love yourself for feeling angry, then surrender it to Source. If you are feeling sorry for yourself, love yourself for falling into self-pity and then hand it up to

Source. If you are indulging and self-sabotaging, love yourself as you notice your behavior and then give it to a higher power. As soon as you get down on yourself, you have lowered your vibration and have separated yourself from the good feelings that you so long to experience. You are cutting yourself off from the very thing you want to have. You are also pushing against who you are, which will only keep the emotions around a bit longer, until you remember that you <u>do</u> know how to change the way you think and therefore feel.

I know in my own life that when I find myself lapsing into frustration or fear the quickest way out is to start saying "Thank you" to the universe for my fear "Thank you for my frustration. I love myself anyway and even though I am feeling these feelings I happily surrender them to Source." As I appreciate that these emotions are perfect and are offering me an opportunity to not push against them, and as I open to embrace them, they magically disappear. Which is not to say that the same or different emotions will not be triggered again. There will be reactions until you are whole within yourself. Until you are so connected with your Source Energy and happy with yourself, that you do not need to be reactive any more. In this centered space you will lovingly see from an overview, without reacting from your ego/personality.

Finding and allowing the flow of joy allows you to see with unclouded eyes that all is as its meant to be. You will find yourself in a place of being able to suspend judgment and blame. You will know that each person is working through their own karmic situations, doing the best they can with what they have. It becomes apparent that it is not our place to believe that we know how others should think and feel.

As you read this chapter you may feel a million miles away from living in joy. Yet it is an ongoing process, that as you awaken and become more aware of how you feel, leads you towards having this experience as your reality.

Release the idea that you are right, and see how your world becomes more joyful.

Let's look at a few ways that we disconnect from a joyful energy. Your thoughts create feelings, and different thoughts have different beliefs attached to them. These beliefs create within you feelings that may be enjoyable or uncomfortable, depending on whether the thoughts are in harmony with your Inner Wisdom or your ego.

Everything you do and think, has a belief of one sort or another attached to it, and many of your beliefs create great stress and anguish in your lives. You may spend hours a day thinking about how others should live their lives, how they should behave and think. How you know what is best for them, if only they would listen. Or you push yourself to achieve more, do more, be more. More than what? Are you forgetting that you already are perfect, exactly as you are meant to be at this moment in your life. For who you are and the way you are right now, paves the way for who you will be in the next moment. Yes, you probably have forgotten. And what's worse is that you immerse yourself in self-reproach about your behavior, and judgment of others, and leave even less room for the feelings of joy and happiness.

What you judge in others is what you judge in yourself.

We have already talked about taking responsibility for yourself and your thoughts, so its time for you to think about an area of your life that is giving you pain or frustration in some way. Is it connected to someone else? Do you blame someone or something for the way you feel about it? Have you rationalized that if they

176

were different or your situation was different you would be happy? Have you told yourself that none of it is your fault, that you are just a pawn in this game? Now, for a moment remember that nothing is in your life by chance. Everything is here with you because you have invited it in—everything!

Look at your situation from your Inner Wisdom perspective, and ask yourself a few questions.

Whatever you feel about someone else, turn it around and ask yourself if its true of you. For example: If you think others should be more considerate of your feelings, go within and ask yourself.

- "Should I be more considerate to others or to myself?" Take a moment to let yourself answer from a deep level within, and you will find most often it turns out to be true. Another thought might be.

- People are not to be trusted for they constantly let you down. Go within, and ask if you trust yourself to be true to you. Do you let yourself down when you don't live up to your own expectations? Do you let other people down?

- If you feel that people don't respect you enough, do you really respect yourself? Do you respect others?

Any feelings that you carry about yourself that keep you feeling less than wonderful will affect your ability to manifest. It will not stop the manifesting process, but what will you be manifesting if the stronger energy is laced with not feeling very good about yourself?

Although many of us are not clearly attuned to our Inner Wisdom, the more you accept that you have this built in guidance system the quicker you can develop a sensitivity to utilize this gift.

Perhaps by now you are more aware that your passionate thoughts are always creating. Whether you are unconsciously sending out energy in the form of thoughts that create negative emotion, or consciously visualizing and affirming, it is the same. Your worry, anxiety, and fear, will find their equal match and return to you more of the same, as will your conscious desire for happiness, joy, and abundance. The universe continually works to give you what you are focused on.

Right now make a decision to connect with joy, even if you don't know how. Imagine that you have a magic wand inside you that offers you this opportunity. Change your thoughts from fear to trust and hope. Pretend that you feel good. Pretend that your life is filled with beauty and wonder. Imagine and pretend that you already are connected to the wonderful feelings you want to be part of your life. As you do it with intensity you will be surprised to see that joy really is there right under your nose. As you pretend, your energy changes. Your vibrations move to a higher frequency and you start to connect with thoughts and emotions that allow you to feel better. You really will believe that everything you want is right there waiting for you to be ready for it. Keep repeating, "I love myself for I am part of Source. As I continue to listen to my intuition and focus on how I want to feel, I allow it to happen. I open to joy, I allow joy to flood through my body. I am ready right now. Thank you Universe."

Chapter Six

RECREATE YOURSELF

What an amazing time we are now living in, where we can finally understand how our thoughts create reality as metaphysics and quantum physics support each other. Now we can see how we have instant change at our fingertips if we believe it is possible. It has been very eloquently explained by Deepak Chopra how 99% of our bodies are constantly renewing themselves, and it is also a fact that we are able to change our thoughts and beliefs no matter what chronological age we may be.

There are so many myths we buy into that perpetuate the idea that once we reach a certain age we can no longer expect to reverse any signs of aging, or change our patterns of thinking and behavior.

Although each of us is programmed with our own genetic coding, we have complete free will to change the way we think and feel. We always have a choice to see a situation with our heart or our ego. As we connect with our hearts we are in harmony with our Inner Spirit following the guidance of our Inner Wisdom. From this vantage point we can conceive a new vision of how we want to be. We can continue to change and grow for as long as we are on this planet, for that is one of the reasons we incarnated in physical form. We have within an ongoing process of awakening that allows us to drop beliefs that no longer serve us, as we continue to open our minds and hearts to new ever expanding ideas. As soon as we believe that anything is possible and we step out of the accepted mass consciousness beliefs about life, we are free.

It is our Divine right to become the person that we want to be. We create and re-create ourselves constantly, although often without much apparent change. As we expand our beliefs and understanding of life we have the vision to see that we no longer choose to recreate ourselves in our old limited image. Now it is time for us to soar in our imagination, and fantasize with passion about who we are becoming.

WHY FIX THE OLD?

The idea of recreating yourself may seem far fetched until you understand how it works. If the subconscious mind does not know the difference between what is real and what is imagined then why let it dwell on unpleasant and limiting thoughts that belong to your past. Throughout your life your memory is like a tape recorder receiving signals from all of your senses, and these memories are stored in your subconscious. Memories have beliefs connected to them that are fleetingly in your conscious mind and then forgotten. These memories stored in your subconscious continue to affect you throughout your life. You will find these memories are triggered by various circumstances that you encounter. But, these situations in your past are only as real as the energy you feed them. The trouble is we usually over feed them! When triggered into re-enactment its so easy to allow your old emotional reaction to encompass you, and when you allow this to happen its almost like becoming unconscious. We seem to completely forget about choice.

If you expect to always react the same way to certain experiences and people, that program in your subconscious will get triggered every time a similar situation occurs. What happened in the past is not real anymore. It is only a memory you hold on to. It is not actually taking place right now, it is only being remembered. How long do you want to go on thinking of yourself in the same old way, with your frustrated feelings of being stuck in a rut, repeating the same old patterns? As you think about the way you are do you feel uplifted or uncomfortable?

If you are constantly looking at what you don't like about yourself you are in a battle with what you want to get rid of. If you feel uncomfortable when you look at how your life is going, ask yourself how long you have been in this battle? Who is winning? Trying to fix the old is similar to putting a Band-Aid on a wound that has not been cleaned. It is covered up, and you don't know what is going on inside until it gets infected and makes itself known to you, or, you take off the Band-Aid and can see that it's not healing.

Clearing old habits of thought and belief does not have to take years of therapy seeing very little change. You control your thoughts. As long as you focus on what is wrong with you and your life, the longer it is going to take you to get where you want to be. You always have the choice to work with your Inner Wisdom, and if you pay attention to your feelings that are connected to certain thoughts, you will be guided very quickly into what feels best and is in your highest interests.

To begin the process of aligning yourself with a different vision of how you want to be, a change of focus is needed. If you know what it is that you would like to be different (and I am sure you do), instead of being upset about what you think is wrong and how you or the situation is not changing, take your focus off the fear and anxiety that you are living with. Focus on what you want to experience. How do you want to be? How do you want to feel?

Make believe that you and your life are right now the way you want them to be.

Remember that the universe and your subconscious do not know the difference between what you are making up, and what is your actual experience. It is the intensity behind your desires that creates change, and the universe responds, rearranging itself. Imagine that you can superimpose a situation of how you want things to be over how they were before, and then place more attention on the change you are desiring. By doing this you shift your focus from what is, as you focus intently on what you are creating—acting and feeling as if it is already a part of your life.

James was with me in the office looking quite down in the dumps. He had decided that he needed a new breath of life in his career. He had been a very successful singer, and over the years had faded from the limelight. I could see psychically that his highest probable future would lead him back into success, yet at the time we were talking, his immediate focus was on all that was wrong in the present.

I explained to him in detail that focusing on what he perceived to be wrong, would only create more of what he wanted to get rid of. James had his focus on not having any hit songs on the charts. The more he thought about his career being over, or at least going downhill, the worse he felt. When you find yourself in a similar situation whether focused on not having enough money to pay your bills, feeling lonely without someone to love, or focused on an illness or disability you are experiencing, you are always sending an energy to the universe that will reinforce your feeling fearful, sad or sorry for yourself. At these times it is easy to feel as if you are drowning in all you perceive to be wrong, and you can barely keep your head above water. This is the time to start imagining a new reality, yet it is also the time when it is the most difficult to increase your vibrational energy to match the changes you want.

First James needed to see that whatever was happening in his career was exactly as it was meant to be. If it wasn't perfect for him in his growth, it would not be happening. His life was showing him that he was not using his energy in a positive way, and being disgruntled he was in effect saying, "Source, you have made a mistake."

As he accepted that there are no mistakes, only constant opportunities to change and grow, he realized how he spent so much of his time dissatisfied and wanting more. For James more was connected with needing to feel he was lovable through the adoration of his fans. His own inner growth had been lost in his ego's gratification received by his popularity. His spiritual growth was on hiatus as he was ignoring his Inner Wisdom. When a "star" falls out of the public eye they are thrown back on themselves, and have the chance to re-evaluate their priorities. Needing outside adulation to help find self love is something a lot of people go through, yet what it is showing you is that you need to recognize that you are lovable and wonderful just because you exist.

Over the next few weeks, James did a lot of soul searching. He started to change his focus from obsessing on what was "wrong" in his life to appreciating what was "right." As he did this, he was sending a message to the universe that he was ready to be a "hit" again. He did his affirmations and visualization when he was feeling in a high clear place. For James, working out in the gym helped him feel that way. He became more aware not to affirm and visualize when he was feeling frustrated or judgmental. Needless to say he passed his own test, which was the most important one. He once more began to skyrocket into the limelight.

James had his own agenda on his path of growth, as we all do. It was in his hands as to whether he passed his own test of ego versus his spiritual growth. We forget what we have programmed for ourselves as we enter the physical realms, yet our plans influence every step of our lives. We have created parameters for ourselves but not exact events. Our free will and ability to co-create determined by our level of consciousness and our chosen karma, decides how much of our predetermined path affects us. The more we learn to transcend our limitations and obstacles and believe that we are unlimited in our possibilities, the greater is our opportunity to realize our potential.

As we think about what we want, the way we want it to be, and imagine it is already available it may seem as if we are making it up. And, initially we are, that is also perfect. Remember the universe doesn't know the difference.) If we are imagining it with intensity and if we believe all is energy and all is possible, the situation we are re-creating in our minds will happen for us as long as we give it enough energy.

To re-invent yourself you need a really
clear picture of where you want to go
and how you want to be.

As you think about re-inventing yourself, imagine the future you. Decide how you want to act and feel as you think about creating a new image of the life you choose to live. As you take time now to create a picture in your minds eye, become aware without judgment of places within yourself that you feel need improvement, areas that keep you stuck, repeating old patterns.

Perhaps you want a new job, a new way to make money. The old you would work at finding the right position. Perhaps you would send out numerous resumes, make many phone calls, and put yourself through all sorts of anxiety with your thoughts. You may think about whether you are qualified, or, what if you are too old, too young or too heavy. Maybe you will not be bright enough or have enough experience. The list can go on and on, and it will probably be a very anxious time for you.

The new you now understands all about energy and thought and creation, so now you have a different way of going about finding a new job. First you send an energy into the universe saying. "I am so grateful for a wonderful new job, one that pays me more than I have ever earned before. Even though I may not know exactly what I want to do, I know it is fun and challenging and creative. I am connecting with the perfect vibration that matches my desire in this area. I ask my Inner Wisdom to fine tune my energy so that a match is found for the perfect job."

By now you will be feeling really good inside, as you think about how wonderful it will be to have a well paying creative way to earn money. You know that somewhere that position that you can fill is waiting for you. You trust that if you keep focused on being in harmony with your desire that the universe will find a way to connect you with the right people. With your new energy, even though you may decide to go out on interviews or contact an employment agency, the phone may ring, and through a seeming coincidence a friend may tell you about a job opening they heard about.

The old you would feel that you had to <u>make</u> it happen. You would work at getting the job, and would believe that you and only you are responsible. The new you would also know its up to you to create that perfect position in a far easier way as you attune your vibrational energy flow. The more work you do on an energy level imagining the perfect position as yours, the more the universe rearranges itself to bring it to you. No matter what you want to have in your life, this is a far easier way of attracting it than the old fashioned way of struggle, as you tried to make it happen.

So how does the new you dream of being? Maybe you see yourself as strong, loving, centered, happy, creative, spiritual, psychic, trusting, honest, generous, whatever is important to you. You are very aware of the places in your life where the old you feels lack, so use this awareness to change your focus, and let it show you more of what you want to create in the new you. Visualize how you would like your surroundings to be. What circumstances you want to experience, supported by what type of people. Write it out if it helps you to focus.

Realize that to recreate yourself you need to be excited about the changes you want to create. So enthuastic that you can feel the excitement coursing through your body.

If you find yourself feeling apathetic as you think about your future, the first thing you will need to reinvent is a future you who is alive and excited about changing your life. If you find yourself thinking that this is just your imagination, remember that someone's imagination is where all the things we see and touch began.

Close your eyes and think about what how you want to be, give this picture as much sensory input as you can, really letting your body participate in feeling as if you are this new you. Become aware of how it feels. Does it feel positive and comfortable? Or do you find resistance inside yourself? Are you aware of uncomfortable feelings?

If there are any feelings that do not feel right you know that you still have a hidden agenda, some belief somewhere that you have not yet uncovered that is not allowing you to accept change. Do you believe that you have the ability to recreate yourself? Do you expect that you can co-create or do you doubt it will work? Sometimes fear will surface as you recreate yourself. After all, you know yourself the way you have been, yet you don't know yourself the way you imagine being. This is ego trying to hold on to the old you, and it is stopping your growth. So just understand that, and treat it like a little frightened child. Send it love, and affirm that you intend to change in a way that will benefit all aspects of who you are.

You are asking a major change of yourself to let go of who you think you are, which is based on who you think you were. It is quite a radical concept to tell yourself that your past is not "you." The past is your memory of circumstances, experiences and feelings, and how you related to them at that moment—but is not who you are right now. Who you were last year and the memories that allow you to think back and identify yourself, are nothing more than memories of certain beliefs that you held then. Memories that allowed you to interpret your life and identify yourself as you created your persona. That is not who you are. Those were last years interpretations of your experiences. And the year before was based on different beliefs and interpretations determined by your mind set at that moment. Who you will be next year is not who you are right now, for your beliefs constantly change and affect what you think you see. You are a powerful force, with ever changing thoughts and beliefs that continue to facilitate your awakening process as you paint your canvas of life with love and joy.

I AM WHO I AM RIGHT NOW

If you can stop dragging your past memory of the way you have been into present time, and identify with that deeper wiser part of yourself, you will experience an enormous sense of freedom. Find the enthusiasm you had as a child as you recreate yourself in this now moment. Tell the universe "this is who I am. " Repeat it three times as you imagine you are born anew right now. Free of all encumbrances that you have been dragging with you in the form of memories of the way you were. Feel the lightness and the sense of freedom that arises from within, for these words are so in alignment with your Inner Wisdom that you will have a feeling of "coming home."

Say it to yourself again, "There is only the me that I am right now." Acknowledge that you are different from the you a minute ago, as you are not that memory.

You are being born anew every minute of every day, and you are wonderful, you are perfect.

Only when you drag who you were based on your judgments and beliefs into present time, can you feel badly about yourself. When you detach from your past, and shift into present time, here you are. Not thinking about your past or your future you feel connected to your Inner Wisdom, and your heart sings.

As you practice repeating this little exercise it will probably be one of he most important thing you can ever do for yourself. Your subconscious accepts that this is the new you, and acts accordingly. As this idea is accepted you will be living from a place that is far more in harmony with your Spirit, than when you were dragging the old you along. Isn't it time to let go of your guilt and your grudges and burdens that have been a part of your make up for so long? Do you really need them to know who you are, or do they only indicate who you thought you were in your past?

As you repeat this exercise throughout your day you will probably hear a little voice telling you that it is impossible to let go of all your memories and expectations of how you have thought and behaved. Once more this is the voice of your ego, so its up to you how much attention you place on it. Wherever you place your focus of attention is where you create reality in present time. "I am new right now, I am joyful, creative, happy, right now in present time." Make this your new mantra and watch how quickly you let go of your old way of being. Change your story in this moment, and create a new one that encompasses all your heart desires, all that brings you joy, right now.

MANY PROBABLE FUTURES

As you work on co-creating your life you will find that Divine timing always has the last word, and its just as well! Can you imagine the pickle we could get ourselves into if we could manifest instantaneously? We could never have a mean thought about anybody without it manifesting, and if it did, we would find ourselves with new negative karma to work through.

As we think thoughts with intensity, we are literally creating different scenes and situations on the causal plane. The causal plane exists in a dimension that is not visible to our naked eyes. It is a place where creations take form on an energy level before they gain in density and become tangible in our present life.

The Universe is constantly rearranging itself
to create different probable futures for you.

Although our passionate thoughts are the ones creating circumstances and events on the causal plane, we have many other thoughts that create less powerful futures. These are paths that will probably not become part of our life. Everyday our thoughts are literally spinning out many different paths creating the future. Yet it is our most intense desires that are without contradicting thoughts that create our most powerful and probable path. If we think of ourselves standing at a point with a few paths in front of us, we see how our choice of thoughts will determine which path we choose to take.

There is no wrong path, only different experiences.

Our choice that we make each and every moment determines which probable future we decide to experience and are ready to explore. We all have a highest probable path that enhances our spiritual growth. That is usually the clearest one I see as I give readings to people. But free will allows us to decide if we are ready to take that particular path into that future. Free will also allows us the freedom to choose another experience first. Eventually our soul will guide us along the path of greatest benefit for our spirit, but many other paths may first be experienced along the way.

IS THERE ANYTHING I CAN'T DO?

The more you strengthen your connection with your Inner Wisdom, the more you realize it is your Divine right to manifest anything you choose. It is important not to harm anybody else and not interfere with another persons life choices. If you want millions of dollars it is your Divine right to have it. If you want to have a wonderful loving relationship, health and wealth you can have it all. If your desire is to become enlightened you can do it. Whatever is in your consciousness to have, you have the tools available to con-

196

nect with it. The universe does not hold anything back from you, judge whether you are worthy or not, or punish you in any way. It only responds to thought and emotion received as energy.

When you get locked into a challenging situation that is happening right now, it is sometimes so hard to believe that your thoughts can really create change. In these times of struggle its so easy to focus on what you decide is wrong, and your focus perpetuates it until its overwhelming. If that is where you are now with any issue whatsoever, stop, and regroup your thoughts and emotions. For whatever you are thinking is "wrong," is only going to stay until you can let go of thinking about it in a negative way. Trust there is a higher purpose in the experience, and imagine the outcome you want.

> *There isn't a second of any day when you are not re-creating yourself on many levels.*

Cells constantly renew themselves, your thoughts are constantly changing, and your experiences are constantly changing. You are never in the same place doing the same thing in exactly the same way. Something, however subtle will have changed. So you are never not re-creating and re-inventing yourself.

When you can really accept this idea, you don't get locked into thoughts such as. "Well this is my reality, and I have to deal with it." Instead you may get on with doing what you need to do, but without anger, or resistance. As you take care of business keep in your consciousness the image of the universe re-arranging itself.

If you are living your life in a way that is not bringing you pleasure, ask yourself. "Is this life the one I want to focus on, or will it help me to feel better if I imagine how I would like it to be?" Simply change the outcome in your mind, and that will start to rearrange energy around the situation you are experiencing. By taking this approach you will certainly allow yourself to have happier feelings flowing through your body. It becomes an ongoing process to take your focus off the small picture that doesn't feel good, and focus on the bigger picture of a situation you are creating that is more uplifting.

Allow yourself to fantasize that your challenges are nothing more than atomic particles of energy floating around that have gathered together to create this situation in your life. When I think about difficult situations this way they somehow lose some of their impact.

You want to create a new life and a new you, so where do you go from here? Start right now by taking your focus off what ever you do not want in your life, and think about how you want it to be. Sometimes it's hard to understand and believe there is more than one reality, yet where you focus your attention is what creates your experience. If you remember that your subconscious doesn't know the difference between what is imagined and what is real, and that the universe is rearranging itself around your thoughts, you may begin to see how your experiences can change. Focusing with enough intensity on the outcome you desire as if its already happened will definitely create change.

MaryJane was overweight, and had been at least fifty pounds over her ideal weight for many years. She believed in positive thinking yet so far had been fighting a losing battle. As we talked I pointed out to her how she was sending out an energy of a future self that was her ideal weight, thinking of herself as thin, yet at the same time she was also sending out an energy with her thoughts that said. "It hasn't worked before, why will it now?" She was so focused on the way she was and had been for a long time, that she was giving that reality more power than her desire to be thin.

We used various techniques such as putting her fears and doubts in the silver box. We worked with her subpersonalities, so that she could leave her cellular baggage behind and start fresh to re-create herself. As soon as MaryJane was congruent in her decision, it was as if she was reborn. She was motivated and sure that "now" was the time. The weight started to melt off her, it was absolutely amazing.

She had held this image of how she wanted to be for so long, but had always unconsciously sabotaged herself with her thoughts of "Yes but" without knowing that she was doing it. Now that she understands how to co-create in a clear way she feels so strong, and has this belief that everything she wants to experience in her life is possible. That is the beauty of learning how to use your power. The more you see results, the more you believe you can do anything.

Ultimately as you continue to re-create yourself, you are peeling away the layers that kept you from remembering your true essence. You continue to move in a direction that eventually brings you home to self, until you are living as that unconditionally loving Being who is one with the universe.

HOW TO FIND YOUR TIMELINES

Are you are a person who is often preoccupied with your future? Do you spend hours thinking and dreaming about how things will be? Do you often allow this future living to keep you out of present time? Or, are you more past oriented? Do you constantly think back and reminisce about the way things were? Do you think about incidents in your past where you hold on to guilt, and beat up on yourself about how you could have done whatever it was better?

You are now ready to find out where your timelines are.

All of us have within our own special way of coding time, which has an impact on how we think and act in our lives. Our brains need a way to know whether we have already done something, or are we planning to do it at some future date. To find out where clients timelines are before we start the process of recreating I ask them to think about something that is a habit they do everyday. Something they have done, do now, and will do in the future.

Take an example of brushing your teeth. Now close your eyes and think about brushing you teeth six months ago. As you think about this action I want you to witness yourself brushing your teeth, as if you are watching yourself on a television screen, or in a picture frame. It does not matter where you were doing it, and it does not have to be a specific day. You know you did brush your teeth in the past and I want you to sense where you are seeing or feeling this picture of you in your past. It may be to your left, or to your right, or it may be in front of you. It may be close to your body or far away.

When you have a sense of where you placed that image, now think of brushing your teeth today. Once more place the image in a screen of some sort and watch yourself brush your teeth. Where do you have a sense of that picture? Again, it could be to your left, right on in the middle. Now repeat the process as you think about brushing your teeth in the future. Once more find the location of where you sense that picture.

There is no wrong place to have a past, present or future, yet when you know how you have coded time, it does tell you some things about yourself and how you go about life. Most people will have their past on their left (unless you are left handed and then it may be reversed), their present in front of them, and their future off to the right.

Some people are not allowing themselves to even see a future, and often have their past and present in almost the same space. When a person has this configuration of timelines they are usually dragging their past into their present and that means holding themselves back–probably going nowhere fast! If by any chance you cannot find your future, or if it is in the same space as your present, you are limiting your vision, and probably don't expect much to change in your life.

Timelines can be moved around, and are only an indication of how you have been organizing time in your own life up until now.

As you recreate yourself in the next journey you will have the old you on the side of your past, and the future you coming from your future side. If by any chance you are having difficulty determining your timelines don't worry, just make a decision about which side you choose for your past and choose the opposite side for your future.

JOURNEY TO RE-CREATE YOURSELF

You need to give yourself about fifteen minutes of quiet time to do this exercise, and you can either be sitting or lying down.

Relax yourself by watching your breathing, and gradually slow each breath down, and allow your focus to turn within. Imagine a very beautiful and safe room for yourself where you are comfortably sitting in a chair. On the side that represents your past you are going to imagine that another you is materializing. Think about all the fear and beliefs and old habits of thought that this aspect of you lives with daily. Feel this part of you as powerfully as you can. If you are visual also see yourself, and notice the heaviness in your emotional body.

On your future side or perhaps in front of you let another aspect of you appear. This image of you is going to have whatever you want to have inside and out. You can see them as loved and loving, happy and abundant in all areas of their life. Now imagine that the universe is constantly in motion and is rearranging itself around the energetic thoughts that both these aspects of you are sending out. As you look at yourself on the side of your past, you realize that the thoughts this part of you is sending out are creating more of the same old stuff. Old habits and patterns are being re-enacted year after year. Look to the aspect of you that is your future self, and also imagine the universe in constant motion rearranging itself on a sub-atomic particle level around the dynamic thoughts this aspect is sending out. Notice how much lighter the emotional body of this future you appears, and how clear and focused you appear to be.

You now have a choice as to where you wish to focus your energy. Is one of these aspects of you more real than the other, or does it depend on where you place your focus? Which choice do you make, and where do you want to focus your attention? Each image is as real as you decide it is. The universe does not know the difference between how you think you are and how you want to be. It only responds to energy.

Imagine that there are ropes attached to the old you, and see or feel yourself detaching them lovingly. Now turn to the new you and open your arms as you embrace this joyful, creative, loving aspect of yourself into your heart. Feel the merging as your own vibration becomes infused with new focus and desire and a greater connection to Source. Thank the Universe for the way you feel, "right now."

Chapter Seven

THE VOICE OF INNER WISDOM

Your inner wisdom speaks to you through your intuition. You are listening to it when you get a "hunch" about something or someone. Its often a gut level feeling that does not always say the same thing as your logical mind. This little voice can be fleetingly heard as you are about to lock your keys in the car, but so often you don't pay attention to it until you come back to your car and see your keys sitting on the seat. This Inner Wisdom is always guiding you on matters that are big and small, it makes no difference what the issue is. Your Inner Wisdom always supports you speaking through your emotions and feelings, as it gently guides you up a pathway to peace and joy.

Some of you may not hear or feel your connection with your Inner Wisdom, yet it's always available to you. If you pride yourself on your intellect and logic, you may find yourself disconnected to your subtle feelings. It is often accepted that if you are in the world of business your focus needs to be on decision making from a logical place, and the brainier you are the more you are respected. This often brings about disrespect for intuition or gut feelings, and these emotions are often down played. Yet, if you are one of those people who is not in touch with how you feel, have you ever had a time when you wished you had another source of guidance? Have you entertained the thought that perhaps there is another way to get answers besides trying to analyze your way through situations?

Your Inner Wisdom is connected to Source, and as you attune to this voice, you give yourself a beautiful gift.

Inner Wisdom is not something that is metered out to the special ones who have "behaved." Your intuition has always been with you since you were born, and it patiently waits for you to make your connection with it. Your Inner Wisdom loves you unconditionally, and is with you to help create a joyfully rewarding life. It is a connecting energy between your personality and Source, and has only your highest good in mind. It assists in your awakening, healing and aligning with all that transports you into peace and joy. It gives greater guidance than any outside teacher ever could, for it knows you best. It is constantly guiding you using your emotions, as it lets you know if you are co-creating a life that is uplifting, rewarding, and joyful, or one of more struggle.

Two questions I hear the most are: "What is my intuition?" and "how do I know whether I am listening to my intuition or my ego?" If you are waiting for a fanfare of trumpets before your intuition speaks to you, you will be disappointed. You may miss the quiet knowingness, as this clearer part of you gently sends its wise guidance to you. The guidance most often consists of energetic impressions that are felt, heard, or sensed, and are then translated into a comfortable form of acceptance with which you are familiar.

The easiest way to know if you are receiving from your Inner Wisdom or your ego is to notice your feelings. Whenever you are receiving thoughts that are uplifting and have a sense of peace about them, they are from your Higher Self and will be in harmony with your greater well being. This little voice heard through your senses, is letting you know that you are receiving clear wisdom, and it is guiding you into choices that will bring you happiness.

Whenever you are listening to your ego you may think it is the voice of intuition. If it is from your ego, somewhere inside you will feel uncomfortable, and definitely not peaceful. As you go about accomplishing whatever it is you want to do, you may feel as if you are pushing, instead of allowing it to happen easily. If you are in doubt, as to which voice you are receiving—question its validity. Anything from your ego will give you a very different feeling than guidance from your Inner Wisdom

The more you practice listening to your feelings, the easier it is to differentiate between your ego and intuition. It is so clear when you just ask. "Am I feeling uplifted and comfortable, and is the guidance telling me something that will benefit all concerned? Or, will it be negative for someone else who may be involved?" Messages and guidance from your Inner Wisdom are always uplifting, whatever the situation you are asking about.

Often I find myself wanting to hear an answer the way I want it to be, especially if it has an emotional charge behind it. At those times I don't ask for guidance as I know I am not clear enough to hear it. I go to a place of trust that all is for my higher good, instead of trying to psychically "know" what to do. If you carry beliefs and expectations about how your questions are going to be answered, you will often miss the subtle responses that are being sent to you by your guidance, but, you will hear your ego which has a very loud voice.

When it appears that you are not receiving the guidance you asked for, you may feel as if you only have yourself to depend on. At times like this you may feel so alone in trying to make something happen. Bear in mind that your Inner Wisdom never leaves you, the guidance is always there. You are always surrounded by your own personal guides, and angelic beings who are with you on this journey of your soul. You have and always will have access to their Higher Wisdom. They are aspects of Source Energy, just as you are, but without their emotional body/ego influencing them, their perspective is clearer than ours. When listening for your guidance, be open to receive it from a casual conversation, a dream, a book you happen to pick up, or from your mother-in-law. Don't limit where it will come from–just trust you will receive it.

ATTUNING TO YOUR INTUITION

Perhaps some of you are wondering how to fine tune your connection with your Inner Wisdom. Isn't it so inviting to think about an open line of communication with this built in teacher. For me it has been wonderfully healing and uplifting to accept that every minute of my life my intuition is guiding me. It really is exciting to realize that your Inner Wisdom is a part of you. Not some Being sitting on a cloud waiting for you to get "spiritual" before it connects with you.

You don't need to change your behavior to have this wonderful part of you be your support system. Just tune in and pay attention to that little voice within that allows you to feel discomfort if you are doing something that is not in your higher interests. It is the voice of warning that so often nudges you when you are not sure about someone you may be doing business with. Those times when you know you feel uncomfortable and are not sure about their integrity, even though logically everything checks out.

Alice was a lawyer and took great pride in being very intelligent and honest. She enjoyed defending the under dog, and when she came to me she was about to take on a new case. It was a father who had been accused of sexually molesting his daughter. Alice was sure he was being maligned by his wife as he had recently requested a divorce, which she did not want to grant him. Alice did not come to me about this issue, yet as I psychically tuned into her, the accused mans energy came into her reading. When I asked her about him, she told me the story. I asked her if she felt that he was innocent of the charge, and suggested that she check with her innermost feelings and not just her head. Alice admitted she felt uneasy when she listened to her Inner Wisdom guidance about him. I suggested that she listen to that little voice of intuition!

It was about three months later that Alice came for another session, and she was quite distraught. She had become fairly involved in the life of her client, and it turned out that DNA testing had proven him to be guilty. Alice did not want to make the same mistake again, and wanted to learn how to trust her intuition. She soon learned how to place herself in a meditative state and connect with her Inner Wisdom. She has since become quite psychic, which is a great tool for a lawyer to develop. It wasn't that Alice made a mistake by not listening to her Inner Wisdom. By having that experience it became a learning process that allowed her to expand her beliefs, and begin to utilize the tools that had always been with her.

As you ask your intuition to become more obvious to you, notice the times when you are thinking about someone you may not have seen for a while. Perhaps you run into them in the market, or someone mentions them to you. Or maybe the phone rings, and you intuitively flash on the name of the person who is calling you before you pick it up to answer it. Just pay attention to how many times a day you do notice a gentle guidance.

Your intuition is very diligent about helping you to take the highest path that will offer you the most joy, if only you will listen, To hear clearly means that you need to move your loud ego out of the way so that you can hear the gentler messages that are guiding and supporting you. The more you acknowledge the times when you notice your intuition, the stronger it becomes. Its like a muscle that hasn't been used–it responds to exercise and stimulation.

EGO VERSUS YOUR INNER WISDOM

Your Inner Wisdom does not want you to learn the hard way. It doesn't want you to suffer unnecessarily. It is your ego that creates difficult and challenging situations for you. One way of thinking about your ego is to think of it as an aspect of you that is primarily concerned with your survival in your physical body. It loves to be in control. In fact its very survival depends on it controlling you, and making sure that you do not change too much. It wants to make sure that you keep listening to it as it dictates to you about fear, limitation, and lack.

The strength of your ego is determined by you. You can feed it, and let it become completely obnoxious, or you can humor it as if it were a little child. Your ego is an energy and an idea that you have accepted as real, when in actual fact it is all illusion. It doesn't have any more control over you than you allow it to. Your ego wants you to give your attention to the life that is going on around you. To see through unclear eyes that are affected by your past experiences and your beliefs about what you have experienced. Your ego is always trying to divert your attention from your own inner awakening by keeping you dependent on it. And, it certainly doesn't want you to pay attention to your intuition.

If you are having difficulty listening to your Inner Wisdom here are a few beliefs that might be affecting you.

- A belief that there is no such guidance.
- Believing that you are not worthy of being guided towards happiness.
- It is wrong to connect with "things" not of this world.

Inner Wisdom connected to Source knows you completely, for it is who you are in your wholeness.

Have you ever thought what it would be like to be loved absolutely and unconditionally. You may have heard your whole life about earning love, or remember being told as a child that you will only receive gifts from Santa Clause if you are "good " and behave the way the adults want you to. Somehow in parents minds, children doing what they are told to do means they have earned the right to be loved. After experiencing this type of conditional love all of your life, is it difficult to believe that you deserve to be loved just because you exist? And beyond that, because you are love itself? Your wonderful Inner Wisdom is always with you, to remind you by its prompting that you are being loved unconditionally. It doesn't matter what you do or don't do, you are being constantly guided towards a greater happiness– if you listen.

The second that I begin to feel a negative emotion I am now aware that my Inner Wisdom is saying, "Aileen change your thoughts, unless you want to create something that becomes a lesson for you." Once upon a time, when I was not aware of the reasons why I was not feeling happy, and I just knew that "something" was wrong, I used to get hit over the head by the universe creating a situation that was very painful or challenging. Now I listen to the subtle feelings, and take notice of my thoughts that are creating these negative emotions, as I would rather learn and grow the easy way. I do <u>not</u> want to be hit over the head by a two by four when I have a choice to avoid it!

As you strengthen your connection with your Inner Wisdom and follow its guidance, you begin to experience synchronicity in your life.

As you listen to your Inner Wisdom you will know that you are creating what you want to experience as you feel uplifted in your thoughts and affirmations. You will be gently guided to pay attention to what is going on around you. When you have a question that you want answered, ask your intuition for guidance and then keep your eyes and ears open. Its amazing where you sometimes receive answers from. Know that you will always receive an answer, for your Inner Guidance knows no judgment. You don't have to earn a connection with this wonderful teacher for it lives in unconditional love.

As you strengthen your connection with this masterful guidance you begin to move beyond a life of beating up on yourself for not living up to your own expectations. You realize that those judgmental feelings towards yourself or others are only creating more of the same, and that is the last thing that you want to perpetuate.

Gradually you find your heart expanding in love and understanding as you free yourself from thoughts that create disharmony in your Being. You become much more forgiving and expanded in your thinking. As you attune to your Inner Wisdom, you connect with the creativity of the universe. Whatever you do in life becomes enhanced as you become more creative, joyful, and loving. Mothers and fathers become better parents, husbands and wives become closer and wiser. Writers, artists, singers find an added dimension in their work. Yes, everyone benefits, no matter what job you may be doing, and life becomes better.

This is a story of how Carlos' intuition saved him from a very serious car accident. He recounted this story in one of our workshops. He was on the freeway driving home from work one day, feeling quite happy with himself, listening to music and singing. He was in the right hand lane and traffic was fast and smooth. He was not really in a hurry, for he had left enough time to get home and be on time for his date that night.

Suddenly he had the strongest feeling that he must exit the freeway, and his body began to feel fear. He felt most uncomfortable yet it was an irrational thought as there was no traffic backup and he needed to get home. He began to feel physically ill, and again he was overwhelmed with the thought that he had to get off the freeway. By now he was feeling so nauseous that he decided to go to the nearest gas station. Carlos started to take the next exit available, and as he slowed down on the exit ramp a big rig careened out of control, crossed into the lane he had been in and smashed into the car that had been in front of him. He may have lost the contents of his stomach at that moment of watching the accident, but his Inner Guidance had saved his life.

Since that incident he has been very motivated to listen to that little voice of intuition, and pays attention to how he feels as much as he can.

This wonderful friend is always with you as well, all you have to do is to deepen your connection with this unconditionally loving part of you. It is your protector and your ever loving guide, and with a little practice you will begin to hear and sense it in a clearer way.

In a less spectacular way, as you listen to your emotions and pay attention to how you feel, you are having an ongoing conversation with your Inner Wisdom. Remember that anytime you feel negative or out of sorts, you are reinforcing something you don't want. To change your thoughts is simply a matter of saying or thinking something in a different way. Anytime you focus on what you don't want you will have a completely different feeling to the one you will have as you focus on what you do want. Even though both thoughts want the same outcome they will not create it! One of the easiest ways to listen to your intuition is to sit quietly and meditate for a few minutes. As you quiet your mind, you make space to receive the signals from your Inner Guidance.

JOURNEY TO CONNECT WITH
YOUR INTUITION

Find a comfortable place to relax and begin to take a few deep breaths. Allow your consciousness to turn within as you let go of the outside world. Imagine yourself being lifted up as if you are being cradled in two large, safe, loving hands. You are being lifted higher and higher, and as you focus on your third eye at the bridge of you nose you feel as if you are beginning to spiral upwards as you imagine yourself floating higher and higher. In your minds eye imagine a beautiful angel appearing in front of you. You may see, or sense, this wonderful presence calling you towards a path that meanders through the trees. Happily follow this angel towards a large shallow clear pool of water. As you come closer to this large pool you are amazed at the magnificence of the celestial colors that are reflecting in its shimmering light. It is water like you have never seen before; it has a clarity and beauty that is beyond words. It is a sacred pool, a pool that you are being invited to step into.

Your angel asks you to think of all the reasons why you may feel unworthy of connecting with your intuition. Go deep within and let the emotions float to the surface of your awareness. Perhaps you feel that you are too negative or unworthy in some way. Maybe you are waiting until you are "perfect" enough. Whatever your excuses and reasons, you are going to take them into the magic pool to be washed out of you.

Step into the water, into the rainbow of beautiful colors, and feel the liquid caress your body. The temperature of the water is perfect for you, so safe, so secure, as you allow the water to flow over your body. Imagine all of your negative feelings are releasing into the water. All of your excuses that have kept you repeating old negative patterns all of the habits of thought that you are ready to change, are being flushed out of you. As you step out of the pool you are clothed in robes of light, filling you with radiance as they cradle your body.

If you have a decision to make about something in your life, formulate it in your mind. Using your imagination now visualize two paths ahead of you. One path is to your right and one to your left. Make a choice about your issue and put it on one of the paths, and notice what happens. Does this situation look bright, and does it feel good, or does it feel and look dark or blocked? Now put the alternative choice on the other path and see and feel how it looks. Again, is it bright and clear, and does it have good feelings connected to it, or is it dark and uncomfortable? Pay particular attention to your solar plexus area. Any sign of nausea connected with one of your choices is a definite warning signal. Your intuition will guide you to choose the path that is in your highest interests. This journey bypasses your ego and connects you to Source Energy.

Chapter Eight

THE PERFECTION OF NOW

By now you are probably taking responsibility for all that is happening in your life–and all that isn't! So maybe your stuck places are literally the universe offering you ways to take your own power and become whole. Try and find a place within yourself that can say, "Thank you for my struggle, pain and conflict, I see it is offering me a new perspective to understand where I have been tripping myself up." When you reach this place of understanding, you are no longer pushing against what you don't want, and blaming other people for what is not right with you. It is entirely up to you how you act and react in any situation. Remember that you always have the opportunity to put the person and situation into the light with blessings, or you can choose to do the opposite. If you choose to judge, blame and condemn others, those actions and beliefs will perpetuate unfinished business with them that will need to be balanced at a future date. Whenever you fall back into blaming others for difficulties you may be experiencing, you are giving away your power by focusing on someone else having more control in your life than you do.

Only understanding and forgiveness will
allow you to find the freedom and peace
you are searching for.

Sometimes when you are experiencing a particularly difficult period in your life that contains pain or
fear, it is easy to feel very alone. At these times it is
challenging to see how the trauma you are going
through is perfect for you in the moment. In fact you
may find yourself with a built in reaction to fight
whatever you are not happy with. You may decide that
you can overcome, or change anything by sheer force,
if you are determined enough. This way of using your
will power to try and make change happen is very
exhausting, and doesn't usually bring any peace of
mind—it is called struggle.

Your struggle starts with thoughts about how
something should or should not be, followed by your
emotions connected to whether you believe something
is okay or not okay, and then you take some kind of
action based on your beliefs. Your thoughts about each
event in your life either brings peace or creates uncomfortable feelings. If you remember that you have a built
in guidance system, as you listen to your Inner
Wisdom it will let you know instantaneously through
the way you feel, whether your thoughts are in harmo-

ny with the bigger picture of your life. Pain will come from listening to your personalities ideas of how to think and react, and harmony comes from following your inner guidance. Which will you choose?

As you open your heart and expand your mind, you are accepting the idea that everything that comes into your life is something you need. Even if it is something you don't want, it is offering you some type of opportunity. If it is a confrontation, you have the choice to see it from your higher perspective and respond accordingly, or react from your ego and create more negativity in your life.

Whatever situation you find yourself in is <u>always</u> there for your highest good, and is often the most challenging, especially when you are balancing karma with other souls. From the overview, it is possible to see how everything is so perfectly choreographed. Yet, from your emotional self perspective it is so hard to see that inherent in every situation there really is a choice of how you react. You have the option to accept responsibility for having co-created the circumstance and to be grateful for what it is showing you, or do the opposite. From this place of accepting that you do have choices, you can now decide the best way to transcend reactive energy. You can use the situation to become more loving, or, you have the opposite choice to point the finger, blame and complain.

NO MORE PUSHING AGAINST

Deana was going through a very challenging situation with her teenage daughter Beth. She was at her wits end, and didn't know what to do next. Beth was very bright and had always done well in school. And, for most of their life together they had been able to communicate in a way that they both seemed to be satisfied with. About six months after her fifteenth birthday Beth started to change, and they found themselves going through a lot of arguments about various situations. Issues such as an appropriate time to be home, or how much make up was acceptable became major battles, and mother and daughter began to feel estranged from each other.

Deana began to worry. She was creating negative scenarios in her head about Beth's behavior. She was making herself thoroughly miserable as she kept imagining all sorts of horrible situations that her daughter might get herself into. The more fearful she became the more pressure she was putting on Beth and the more angry they became with each other.

As I explained to Deana how her thoughts, especially because they were so emotionally charged were creating more of the very thing she was afraid of, she began to see she had been doing the very opposite of what was needed to create the outcome she desired. As we focus on what we think is wrong with someone, we are reinforcing that very behavior. It was not Deana's situation with Beth that was the real problem. It was the out of control imagination of Deana pushing so hard against her daughters behavior. Her fear was acting like a magnet, attracting more fear based thoughts and feelings back to Deana. The more she worried, the more she pushed for her daughter to change, the more nothing but separation and a battle of wills was happening.

Deana began to see that the quickest way to change a situation that was not useful to either of them, was to see her daughter in her wholeness. She decided to spend a few minutes each day and imagine Beth being responsible and happy, loving and open towards her mother. She visualized them both coming to an agreement where there was compromise on both sides. As she practiced holding this vision and creating it in her mind her affirmations were similar to this: "Divine Universe, in this now moment I am holding a vision of a loving and close relationship with my daughter. I release my ideas of how she has to be, and I surrender all of my negative fears to you. As I fill my heart with loving feelings, I know that I can trust my daughter to do what is best for her. I release all expectations of how she needs to be, and I turn it over to you God to be resolved in its highest form that will benefit all concerned. Thank you."

It was amazing to Deana how quickly Beth began to change. They both agreed that they wanted to find a middle ground that created harmony in their relationship. The outcome was that Deana became more lenient and trusting of Beth, and Beth did not need to act out to prove her independence.

As long as Deana had continued to focus on all she was afraid of, she would have continued to experience a lot of anxiety. She needed to remain caring, but relinquish control. Whenever you are pushing against what is in your life as if it is a mistake, you are creating and perpetuating a situation that feels more like hell than heaven. Deana found out how much she preferred harmony!

Everything that is in your life is exactly
as it is meant to be otherwise it
would not be with you!

If you are not enjoying your experience you certainly don't have to pretend that you like it, but, it does show you there is something in your thoughts, whether conscious or unconscious that still needs healing. Somewhere you are still sending out negative signals that bring situations to you for your growth, and the universe will continue to do this, until you "get it." Sometimes I throw my hands up in frustration and ask the universe. " When? When will I get it?" Then I come to my senses.

Your spiritual acceptance of whatever is in your life allows you to see more clearly where you want to go, yet allows you to be grateful for "what is." It is your way home to all that your heart and soul long for.

THE "THANK YOU" GAME

Sometimes its really challenging to change your energy so that you are congruent on all levels. In other words, its necessary to match your desire with your conscious and subconscious thoughts, as well as in your emotional and physical body. One of the quickest ways to change your feelings so that you can move from trying to make things happen to allowing the match up, is to play the game of gratitude. To begin this process you start by thanking the universe for everything that you see around you. "Thank you universe for my eyes that can see. Thank you for the roof that is over my head. Thank you for the blue sky and for the birds that are singing in the trees. Thank you for my dog, husband, wife, cat or children." Now throw in a "thank you" for something that has not yet manifested in your life. "Thank you for my raise, or thank you for my soulmate, or thank you for my improving health or my feelings of joy." Then continue with, "Thank you for the clothes I am wearing, and for my voice, and my chair that I am sitting on."

As you continue to look around and let the universe know how appreciative you are of all that is in your life, two things are happening. The first is: you are sending out a vibration of positive energy that will attract to you more of all you are grateful for. Secondly your subconscious is accepting your grateful energy, and as it doesn't know what is already here and what is in your imagination, it goes to work sending out magnetic energy to connect with more of all that you are appreciating.

Source does not make mistakes.

It is probably now apparent to you how important it is to think more positive than negative thoughts. As you become more and more aware each time you have a pessimistic or cynical dialogue with yourself—stop. Then change the dialogue to focus on what you want. As you consistently catch your negative self chatter, and turn it around, you will eventually reach a point where your positive thoughts reach a critical mass level. When you reach this stage your thinking automatically becomes focused on positive outcomes. As you begin to think positively about all you want to manifest, you will feel a lightness within you. As you begin to vibrate at a higher frequency, it places your whole being into a state that feels really good. And as you continue to say thank you for what you can see in your life, it has a magical way of changing your focus from what you consider to be wrong, to what is right.

Practice uplifting thoughts and affirmations such as. "In this now moment I appreciate all the wonderful things I have in my life, even as I ask to feel happier and stronger so that I attract more wonderful things that enhance my joy of life and allow me to have a greater peace of mind." Or, "I am so grateful for all the good that is in my life, and I know that everything I am going through I have co-created into my life for a purpose." And finish it with, "all that I am experiencing is showing me that I have a greater vision of how I want my life to be, and I now send this vision out into the universe to manifest as my reality, allowing me to live my life with ease and joy."

As you say the words that sum up what you desire to have in your life, it is really important that you have a very light hearted attitude. By keeping it light you are not sending out double messages that contain an element of fear or anxiety that may counteract what you are co-creating. Whatever you do, do not say and feel these affirmations as if your life depends on the outcome. Thoughts of, "I've got to have," resonate with the energy of "I don't have," and will cancel out what you are asking for. You need to attune to your Inner Wisdom to trust the process, and believe that all is as its meant to be, even if your ego/personality doesn't believe it. Find that place within that allows you to be grateful for whatever you are feeling.

I know that sounds strange to many of you yet you need to be able to say. "Thank you universe for these stuck feelings," or" thank you for my insecurity or fear." "Thank you for my anxiety." "Thank you for whatever feelings I am feeling for they let me know that I am ready for something different." "I am now ready to connect with the frequency of joy, of love, of safety of peace." Say from your heart whatever is important to you. It enables you to lift your spirits and feel that you are participating in creating a happier life for yourself.

If you believe that you know best, and you cannot bring yourself to a place of feeling grateful, you tend to keep doing the same old things over and over until you finally get it—there is something to be learned here. Try and accept that whatever is happening in your life right now is not a mistake, and you are not being victimized. Ultimately it will become a blessing.

ACCEPTANCE AND FLOW

One of the most important ways to create a state of peace within, is to believe that you are loved unconditionally by Source. To be loved unconditionally means you are not judged, there are no expectations on you, and you do not need to do anything to earn love. You are loved just because you exist. It makes no difference if you are heterosexual or homosexual, meat eater or vegetarian, murderer, or saint. Source does not judge, only humans do that.

It is not your Inner Guidance in your head day in and day out that you hear as criticism, it is only your own thoughts. You are the one who beats up on yourself and decides consciously or unconsciously whether you deserve to be happy or whether you should have some suffering and despair in your life.

If you are ready, try this and see how it feels. *You are absolutely loved without conditions!* Are you able to accept this gift yet? Some people take longer to accept this concept than others, yet as you do, you allow yourself to connect with that unconditionally loving energy that begins to heal your heart and helps you to move into a happier way of approaching life.

Until you are ready to take judgments off yourself you will continue to create struggle and will not hear your voice of intuition.

The chatter in your mind from your ego/personality keeps you from hearing the voice of your intuition, and creates within a feeling of disconnection that throws you out of balance. Some people might worry that if they stop self criticism they might not get anything accomplished. It actually turns out to be the opposite. While you are criticizing yourself you are pushing to accomplish, to overcome, to stop procrastinating, to stop being negative or whatever else you beat up on yourself for feeling and doing. While in this frame of mind, you are sending out opposing signals. One says "I want to change," the other says, "I don't like the way I am." More conflict is created within, giving more reason for self criticism.

Loving yourself as you imagine accomplishing whatever you want to, will energize you into greater accomplishment without opposition. The better you treat yourself, the more productive you allow yourself to be, for there is no punishment greater than not loving yourself, and not allowing yourself to receive the love of Source.

As you trust more and more in the perfection of "now" you realize how it does not serve you to become impatient when what you want does not show up in your time frame. Know that all you want already exists, it is just a matter of the universe rearranging itself to match your pictures of reality. Over the years I have noticed in my own life that my impatience is more pronounced when I have doubts. If I do not have even a hint of doubtfulness, if I just <u>know</u> that something is coming then I seem to have more patience as I trust in Divine timing. We can become more patient when we know its going to be there. If we doubt, then a part of us does not believe and we find ourselves once again pushing against what is. If you find yourself with so much impatience in spite of knowing better, then you could say. "Thank you universe for this moment which is offering me more chances for personal growth, I surrender my doubt and impatience into your loving hands."

Life becomes much easier when you stop creating so much pressure on yourself pushing to be more, and do more. You are going to get where you want to go anyway, and the quicker and easier it is for you to get there as you expand into the perfection of who you are "right now. " When you feel impatient notice it, and love yourself anyway, for as you connect with the vibration of love it is emanating at the perfect frequency to create a spiritual shift within you. Once more all your frustrations become blessings.

Chapter Nine

DIVINE ABUNDANCE

By now perhaps you have found out what piece of your puzzle has been missing, and you know how you can fill the void that you have lived with for so many years. You may have received some deep and wonderful answers as you strengthen your connection with your Inner Wisdom. As you make the shift from believing yourself to be completely physical into a combination of spiritual/physical consciousness, you are now on your journey into wholeness.

It is a challenge, and fascinating to see how we need to keep a foot in both worlds as we open up psychically and spiritually. It's very easy to escape into one realm or the other, and lose the balance. Once you start meditating and connect with your Inner Wisdom, you will find those inner places of peace and serenity can become addictive. Connecting with the flow of Source Energy is so wonderful, and offers us a greater clarity to deal with the everyday challenges of life.

It's so exciting to discover that your thoughts about life are what create a heaven or a hell for you. Your thoughts about how things should be only bring pain and anxiety. Appreciating how they are right now without any attachment to the way you think they should be simply sets you free.

Indeed, now that you know how to co-create, each experience that you encounter strengthens your connection with your Higher Guidance. Your lessons of karmic growth will become easier for you to learn and eventually to transcend, as you view them from your higher perspective and give less attention to your kicking and screaming ego.

By understanding that there is no right or wrong as judgments are released, it is possible to see that everything is energy in continuos motion. With that insight comes awareness that each persons actions are perfect for where they are spiritually along their path. Everyone is writing the script of their lives every minute of every day, and there is no wrong way to write it. Your free will allows you to seemingly make mistakes, which only means you have not quite grasped the lesson that you set up for yourself. So it gets re-enacted again and again until you see it, understand your part in co-creating it, and bless it into the Light.

Connecting with your higher perspective to view all that you experience in your life including ex-husbands, ex-wives and mothers-in-law, allows you to dissolve emotions that act as obstacles to your connecting with the abundance flow. In turn this takes you one step closer to connect with that unconditionally loving place within you.

> *Allow others their own experience,*
> *it is their path to wholeness.*

When you feel anger and frustration, are you able to see it is caused by your emotional attachment to beliefs of how others should think and act? When you find those emotions welling up inside, ask yourself the questions that allow you to see once more that it is your ego that is shouting the most loudly. Remember you do not have to always be right, and that your truth is only your perspective on any given situation, and not necessarily someone else's. Every person has the right to their own experience. When you decide that someone has made a "wrong" choice, you are trying to take away an experience that they need–otherwise they would not be having it. Instead of trying to change someone else, change yourself and broaden the way you think, and reap the benefits.

It helps me too think of everyone as flowers growing in a garden. Some of us are growing in rich fertile soil, others are growing in soil that has not been fertilized and is almost devoid of nourishment. Still others may be growing in the mud that sits in the bottom of the pond. Whatever beginnings you may have, and no matter what type of nourishment you may receive, we are all here to grow until we poke our heads out into the light. Some may find as they grow through the soil that stones block their way, and the hardness of the stones hurts if you push up against them. If you relate to this growth you eventually find out that you cannot force your way through, and you find a way to grow around the obstacles.

The seeds in the pond may not have anything blocking their path, yet it is murky and unclear and frightening not knowing where they are going, until they break through to the surface and see the light. Other seeds are nurtured and loved and have seemingly easy paths to the light, yet are besieged by weeds and insects. We all come into the light at different times, yet we each do it at the perfect time for us. Until we have experienced what another person has gone through to be the way they are, we can never compare our growth with anyone else's, for we do not know what they have endured.

How each person "deals" with events is often where the problem lies, for until an experience is interpreted as "good" or "bad" everything is just an event that is happening. As you begin more and more to release old beliefs that made life so much of a struggle, and as you listen more closely to your voice of Inner Wisdom, the easier your path will become.

Every minute of your day you are being given numerous signs that reflect your beliefs. Your emotions are a reflection of your beliefs

Each reaction to anything that you come across every day is a reflection of a belief that you hold consciously or unconsciously. Your beliefs are arbitrary and usually only get in the way of creating a flowing abundant life. As you use your meditations, affirmations, and visualizations you begin to change your old programs that created struggle in your life.

If you do not change beliefs that no longer serve you, you are creating a future based on your past.

You are not here to exist or tolerate life, you are here to live it joyfully and enthusiastically. As you access Divine Abundance, the present time is your most important time. Right now you are creating your future life. Make a conscious decision to not worry about your future, and agonize about your past.

If you are now ready to believe that <u>anything</u> is possible, to live fully in joy you need to stop dragging your past with you to explain your present behavior and excuse why you have not changed. It is time to stop projecting into the future to the degree that it keeps you from being in the now moment, where all change takes place. Your own empowerment is found in the now , for it is now that you create your future, and now that you release your past. Past and future focus keeps you from listening to your Inner Wisdom that is talking to you right now as it imparts constant guidance.

You are always here, right here with yourself, no matter where you go.

If I am on an airplane and I am sitting in the airport at Los Angeles, I am with myself in my body sitting in the plane. When I land in Hawaii, I am still right here sitting with myself even though I am thousands of miles away from where I took off. It doesn't matter where we go, we are always right here with ourselves. We are either living in harmony with our desires and Source, or we are creating a miserable scene that doesn't bring us peace of mind. The choice is always ours.

Even if you want to you know you cannot leave behind what you don't like by moving to another place. Wherever you go unless you have transcended the need to react, judge and point the finger, you will recreate a similar situation that mirrors back to you all you thought you had run from. You cannot escape. It doesn't work that way, for if it did, you wouldn't learn how to bless and transcend all that keeps you from being whole.

Wherever you go, so does your "stuff."

Jean, was a legal secretary. As we started our session she was very quick to complain about her issues with the co-workers in her office. She told me it was their fault she was miserable. She said they were unkind, prejudiced, and sexist, and the unpleasantness was definitely not her fault. I could see psychically that she also had trouble staying in relationships. When we spoke about it, she said it was because the men in her life were not good enough. We talked about effect and cause and magnetic thoughts, and how what we think draws more of the same to us. Only some of our conversation seemed to sink in. She was much happier pointing the finger, and blaming others.

It eventually surfaced that Jean had moved from office to office always finding the same type of unpleasant people. I asked her to repeat what she was accusing others of, and change the words from "you" to "I." You are unkind to me–I am unkind to me, (when I do not like myself.) You are prejudiced—I feel feelings of prejudice towards you. You have a sexist attitude–I have a sexist attitude.

At first Jean denied that she had these feelings, but gradually acknowledged that it was true. She expected people to react to her in a negative way, and of course its exactly what she got. If Jean didn't have those issues in her consciousness, she would not encounter them in the people she was around.

It is not that prejudice and sexism do not exist, we all know they do. But these issues are not something that becomes a part of everyone's life in the same way that Jean had attracted them. Once she took responsibility for her own prejudice, and began replacing it with understanding using a higher perspective, she set herself free. Jean would now be able to go to another office, and almost surely would not have the same experience that she had dragged with her so many times before.

Its a fact that some of us have chosen easier paths than others for our role in this lifetime, yet we all have the same opportunity to view our lives from a higher perspective. Our lessons of growth that we experience, only affect us to the degree that we are unconsciously co-creating. Then, as we begin to consciously work with our challenges and not against them, we begin to transcend the need to have these experiences at all.

You are your path.

Everything in our lives is allowing us to heal our hearts and find within the ability to love unconditionally. Sometimes during a difficult time we may ask for a sign that we are on the "right path." We seem to think that we need guidelines and structure so that we can gauge whether we are headed in the right direction, signposts along the way that say "keep going," or "wrong way-turn back." If we listen to our hearts, we will know that we are our path, for there is only growth. To think there is a wrong path only creates pain and suffering. How can anything be wrong when "All is Source?"

- **KEYS THAT UNLOCK ABUNDANCE**
- Listen to your Inner Wisdom, and learn to trust it.
- When you point the finger and blame others, reverse it and replace the word "you" with "I."
- When your experiencing something that you don't want, let it create enthusiasm and focus for what you do want.
- Undo belief systems that no longer serve you, question from where do your beliefs originate–from your personal experience or from others.
- Forgive others and transcend the need to be "right."

- Know what you are thinking and feeling at all times.
- Be the gatekeeper of your thoughts.
- Align with your divine abundance within, the source of all prosperity.
- Meditate, affirm and visualize, then surrender it all to the universe.

Remembering your higher purpose sets you free

Knowing one's "purpose" in life seems to be very important to many people, as if that understanding will define who you are and give purpose to your life. Whenever I asked my guidance this question, I always received the same answer, which may be a surprise to you. Although we do have a purpose in life, with lessons of karma and growth, and with a goal of learning to love unconditionally, our main purpose is to be free. Free of attachments, free of being dependent on others for our happiness, free of beliefs that keep us imprisoned and free to live in joy as we ultimately claim our power to be the co-creator of our life in harmony with Source.

Now that you know how to listen to your Inner Wisdom through your intuition, do you feel the excitement bubbling up within as you realize how you can change your life from one of struggle to one of joy and happiness? Learning to love yourself and others, and focusing on what you appreciate instead of what is "wrong" will create enormous changes in the way you live life. The vibration of unlimited potential is always available to you.

To remind myself of this I ask throughout my day. "Am I in this experience in an expanded open state or am I in one of contraction?" If I feel uncomfortable in any way I know that I am shutting out the flow of love. As I open up, and in my imagination connect with "Source," I put a slight smile on my lips, and feel the change coming over me.

Whatever situation I am in I ask myself "How much love can I send to these people and this situation?" I may not feel very loving at all to begin with, yet as I connect with my Inner Guidance, and open my heart so that I move beyond taking other peoples behavior personally, I connect with that all encompassing force of pure love and acceptance that fills my being.

Nothing can stop Gods love for you.

Whenever you allow yourself to slide into negative feelings and listen to your own critical thoughts, as part of Source you are actually denying your connection as you call out for help at the same time. No wonder you disconnect from your Inner Wisdom and listen to your ego's voice. When you are asking yourself to be more loving and understanding, be gentle with yourself, and know that you are ready to give whatever amount of love you can in the now moment. Don't judge whether it is enough, or whether you should give more, just do what you can and love yourself anyway!

In the zoo one day a young rhinoceros was contentedly drinking water from his pool when he noticed an elegant giraffe happily munching the leaves of a tree. She was so slim and moved with such grace that the rhinoceros looked at his own reflection in his pool to make some comparisons. He noticed how wide his stomach was and how big his head was and how short and thick his neck was, and decided that he certainly wasn't graceful. He became very sad and decided that everybody would love the giraffe and nobody would give him the time of day. He began to lose his appetite and he hoped that he would lose weight and look more like the giraffe even though he was still horribly depressed.

After a few weeks each time he looked into the pool he found he looked just the same, perhaps a little thinner but basically he was still a rhinoceros. He decided that he did not want to live, for life was pure hell and he prayed for some help. A wise old eagle perched on the branch of a tree near the rhino and asked him what was the matter, why was he so depressed. The rhinoceros replied, "I am so heavy and ugly and if I look over there at the giraffe I see so much elegance and beauty and no one will love me, and I hate myself." The wise old eagle asked the rhino if people came to visit him in the zoo. He said, "Yes, lots of people come to see me everyday." The eagle said, "You are who you are meant to be and that is a rhinoceros, and people come to see you because they think you are a beautiful rhino and they love you for the perfect shape that is you. The same people may also admire the giraffe but they do not want to see a giraffes neck on a rhinoceroses body, as that would look odd. You are wonderful just as you are."

The rhino looked at all the boys and girls calling to him and talking about him and he began to feel very good inside. "I guess the eagle is right. I am perfect," he thought to himself, "just the way I am. And I love to look at the giraffe, but I don't want to be a giraffe. I am happy being me." The wise old eagle had a smile on his beak as he joyfully flew off into the sunset.

As you awaken each day celebrate in your minds eye as you imagine yourself smiling, and happy, singing and dancing, in love with life and yourself. Imagine being filled with a deep sense of contentment that allows you to appreciate whatever comes your way. Send out an energy that connects you with all your heart desires. Act as if you already have access to everything you could possible think of at your fingertips.

Divine Abundance is only a thought away!

About The Author

Aileen works with people from around the world as an accomplished psychic, and workshop leader. She is the author of "Get off the Karmic Wheel.....with Conscious Ascension and Rejuvenation. She hosted her own radio show for five years, and has her own cable television show "Light Transformation."

Aileen inspires us as we see how our emotional thoughts choreograph our lives. She helps us to gracefully transmute our self imposed karma and move into wholeness. Aileen lives in Malibu with Fred, her husband of thirty-three years.

For more information go to

www.aileennobles.com